HOW TO STUDY LITERATURE

General Editors: John Peck and Martin Coyle

HOW TO STUDY A THOMAS HARDY NOVEL

How to Study

Series editors: John Peck and Martin Coyle

IN THE SAME SERIES

HOW TO STUDY A THOMAS HARDY NOVEL

John Peck

MACMILLAN

First published 1987 by
MACMILLAN PRESS LTD
Houndmills, Basingstoke, Hampshire RG21 6XS
and London
Companies and representatives
throughout the world

ISBN 0–333–41755–0

A catalogue record for this book is available
from the British Library.

13   12   11   10   9   8   7   6
03   02   01   00   99   98   97   96

Printed in Malaysia

For Tom

Contents

General Editors' Preface

Everybody who studies literature, either for an examination or simply for pleasure, experiences the same problem: how to understand and respond to the text. As every student of literature knows, it is perfectly possible to read a book over and over again and yet still feel baffled and at a loss as to what to say about it. One answer to this problem, of course, is to accept someone else's view of the text, but how much more rewarding it would be if you could work out your own critical response to any book you choose or are required to study.

The aim of this series is to help you develop your critical skills by offering practical advice about how to read, understand and analyse literature. Each volume provides you with a clear method of study so that you can see how to set about tackling texts on your own. While the authors of each volume approach the problem in a different way, every book in the series attempts to provide you with some broad ideas about the kind of texts you are likely to be studying and some broad ideas about how to think about literature; each volume then shows you how to apply these ideas in a way which should help you construct your own analysis and interpretation. Unlike most critical books, therefore, the books in this series do not simply convey someone else's thinking about a text, but encourage you and show you how to think about a text for yourself.

Each book is written with an awareness that you are likely to be preparing for an examination, and therefore practical advice is given not only on how to understand and analyse literature, but also on how to organise a written response. Our hope is that although these books are intended to serve a practical purpose, they may also enrich your enjoyment of literature by making you a more confident reader, alert to the interest and pleasure to be derived from literary texts.

John Peck
Martin Coyle

1

Where to begin

It is easy to see why most people enjoy reading Hardy's novels. His plots are absorbing and often exciting, the characters make a powerful impression, and the settings of the novels are both striking and vividly drawn. And yet, despite the fact that you may have thoroughly enjoyed the Hardy novel you are studying, you might find it hard to organise a critical response to the work you have read. There are several reasons why this might be so. Sometimes you can become so involved in a novel that it can prove difficult to stand back and look at it analytically. Again, if you are studying a novel for the first time, you might be unclear about what you should be looking for or commenting on. And there is, too, the further fact that a Hardy novel, like any novel, is a long work with a lot in it. One way round these problems is to turn to critical books for help, but these can merely add to your difficulties. You might discover, for example, that Hardy often structures his novels in the form of a tragedy. As you turn to another critical book, you might find out that Hardy is interested in a process of social change in the rural life of England. What might trouble you is why you failed to notice such things when you read the novel and why your impression of it was so different.

The step from reading to studying

At this point many students give up trying to shape their own response to the work they have read, because they can see little connection between their own experience of the book and the kind of things that appear to be central in criticism. Yet most students know that studying English is only going to be really worthwhile if they can formulate their own view of a text. The major aim of this book is to show you how to move from your reading of a Hardy novel to shaping your own response to that novel. A central point, which will be stressed all the time, is that the best way to build a critical response is to start with a few clear, simple ideas about the novel as a whole and to use these to direct and shape all your subsequent thinking. In other words, build your entire response on a firm foundation.

How, though, do you acquire clear and simple ideas about a novel as a whole? This is the major problem in moving from reading to studying. On a first reading you are likely to be so absorbed in the details of the text that you might miss any sense of a larger pattern in the book. By the end of the novel you may well feel that you are faced by hundreds of pieces of a jigsaw which you cannot piece together into a unified picture. Many students never get beyond this stage; they have a host of piecemeal impressions but lack any confident sense of what the novel as a whole amounts to. This book is about how to move beyond that initial bewildered response.

The first problem is where to start. Well, most of us start a jigsaw by building the frame. A novel can be approached in the same way: if you establish a framework at the beginning of your analysis, then you can begin to fit in all the details of the novel. Can you see how this approach tackles the main problem you are likely to experience with a novel? If you have a sense of the work as a whole to begin with, then all your disjointed impressions of character, setting, style, use of tragedy, or whatever, should start to link together. It is how to make this sort of confident start to your analysis that the rest of this chapter explains: it shows you how to establish a framework which will nevertheless give you a great deal of freedom to shape your own distinctive response to a text. The best way of explaining this is if, for the moment, we forget about Hardy and think about novels in general.

The pattern of novels

The first point to grasp about novels in general is that novelists tend to return to the same issues and situations again and again. What most novels present is the experiences of a number of individuals living in a particular society. Every society has certain values and conventions which it regards as important and most of the people in any society are happy to conform and accept these rules. Sometimes, however, people rebel against the usual way of doing things, particularly when they are young; for example, they might rebel by adopting unconventional clothes and unconventional behaviour. But there are other ways in which people might express their opposition to the general standards of society and how they feel at odds with prevailing values. Nearly all novels focus on just such tensions between society and the people who make up that society, fixing in particular on those individuals who rebel or find it difficult to fit in. The major characters in novels are often caught between a sense of their social obligations and a desire, which at times can be a selfish desire, to be true to themselves.

All of this is most evident in a very common kind of novel referred to as 'an education novel': education novels deal with how rebellious young people grow up and eventually come to terms with the society in which they live. Such novels focus very directly on a tension between the individual and society, but this kind of tension is central in most novels. In some novels it is clearly the individuals who are too extreme in their views and behaviour, but in other novels we should be able to see that there is something wrong in the society presented and so understand why the central characters are alienated or at odds with the established social order.

The pattern of Hardy's novels

The broadest pattern that can be observed in a novel, then, is of some kind of conflict between society and one or more individuals within that society. The sequence of incidents which make up a novel dramatise and illustrate the conflict, and in the course of the work as a whole the major characters either achieve an accommodation with society and its values or find themselves progressively more alienated. Even if you have only read one of Hardy's novels you should be able to see that this pattern can be found in his works. Think about one of the main characters: can you see how that person finds it difficult to fit into the society to which he or she belongs? There is a long line of rebels in Hardy's novels – characters such as Bathsheba, Eustacia, Clym, Henchard, Tess, Jude and Sue – characters who always seem in conflict with the world in which they find themselves. The big picture in a Hardy novel, therefore, is of an individual at odds with society. If you can see this in the Hardy novel you are studying it will give you a frame for exploring the work. Your whole critical response could be built on this foundation alone, as you considered the society presented and the main character presented, and thought about the nature of the conflict between the two.

It is, however, possible to establish more about the general pattern in evidence in Hardy's novels. His main characters are rebels, but not wilfully so; it is just that there is something in their natures that makes it difficult for them to fit in. They can see the advantages of conventional behaviour, but simply do not seem able to conform. And, on the whole, Hardy seems to side with these characters. He seems to recognise that the orderly ways of society can be at odds with an instinctive unruliness in human nature. Time after time Hardy shows us a kind of undisciplined wildness in human nature, and in many ways this resembles an undisciplined wildness in the whole of the natural world. This indiscipline of nature is seen most clearly in the weather in the novels, which is always unpredictable, but also more generally nature is often presented as cruel and destructive. The effect is to suggest that the whole of the natural world runs counter to and is at odds with the order of society. This is neatly summed up in Hardy's presentation of farming: farming is mankind's attempt to cultivate and control nature for the general benefit of the community. As such it is vital, but a change in the weather can mock and destroy all mankind's plans.

Hardy's novels, then, present a wildness both in nature and in human nature which is set against the codes and order of society. More simply, we can say that his novels turn on a society versus nature tension. What we can expect to find at the centre of a Hardy novel is a presentation of the experiences of one or more characters caught between their sense of how they should behave and their natural instincts that make them behave in a different way. What we can also expect to find is that this unruliness in human nature will be linked with a similar lack of discipline and restraint in nature generally.

How does this sense of a pattern in Hardy's novels help me?

An awareness of this society versus nature tension in Hardy's novels should give you a firm foundation on which you can build your reading of an individual novel. It should help you make sense of the incidents that make up the story and help you in your interpretation of particular scenes and details. For example, love relationships are often at the centre of Hardy's novels. You might well enjoy the love story for its own sake, but you also need a way of discussing it. The idea of a society versus nature tension gives you a way in, as there is something in the nature of emotional feelings that runs counter to any idea of disciplined social behaviour. Consequently, it should come as no surprise that the characters in love in Hardy's novels often act in a way that threatens and undermines the social institution of marriage. They are responding to their desires rather than to the demands of society. The pattern is always the same: when we have a marriage featuring principal characters in a Hardy novel, one or other of the partners always rebels against the discipline of marriage, craving freedom or adventure or passion. What should have become clear from this brief example is that an awareness of the standard pattern in Hardy's novels will provide you with a way of responding to every incident in a text. Instead of staring at the text and wondering what this or that detail means, your sense of the basic society versus nature tension in his novels allows you to approach scenes and details of the novels with some confidence as to how to read and interpret them. As a further example, consider the ways in which a Hardy novel ends. More often than not the novels end unhappily. This, however, is something that you could predict. The novels focus on characters who cannot settle down, who cannot discipline their natural instincts and compromise. Yet, whether they like it or not, the characters are caught in a particular society, so repeatedly and inevitably the major characters come to grief in the confrontation.

What we have established so far, then, is that if you look for a society versus nature tension this should help you interpret any scene or detail in a Hardy novel. What might concern you is that using this idea might seem to limit your freedom to develop your own view, but this should not prove to be the case. What I am talking about is a very basic pattern in Hardy's fiction: it is how you fill out this pattern that will make your reading of a Hardy novel distinctive, and all kinds of reading can be built on this solid foundation.

Sometimes, however, rather than being left at liberty to pursue your own line through the novel, you might be called upon to consider a particular topic. In preparing for an examination, for example, you might be asked to consider such issues as Hardy's use of tragedy, or his picture of rural life, or his reliance upon coincidence, or his sense of history. All too often students make the mistake of regarding such things as totally separate topics, writing about them as if they are quite distinct aspects of a novel. What you must appreciate is that all such topics interrelate and are simply aspects of the total pattern of the work. The best way to approach such topics, then, is to investigate them again in the light of the idea of a society versus nature opposition. This will provide you with a way of focusing your impressions, and a way of relating one aspect of the text to all your other ideas about the novel. Consider Hardy's interest in history, for example. Far too often students write as if Hardy just happened to have a curious, rather nostalgic interest in the past. The point about Hardy's interest in history, however, is that he writes with an awareness of how civilisations rise and fall. We can develop that point and make more of it if we make use of our society versus nature opposition. Hardy seems to recognise that any social order is merely temporary; society changes, a whole social order can even collapse, but nature is constant and unchanging. Hardy's interest in history, therefore, is one way in which he brings to life in his work his larger vision of a constant battle between society and nature.

In subsequent chapters I explain how other aspects of Hardy's novels can be approached in a similar way, working from the same simple basic idea. At the moment, however, it is quite possible that the last few paragraphs might have lost you as they anticipate issues that the rest of this book will explore. Let me, therefore, return to the main points that I want to get across here: there is a recurrent pattern in Hardy's novels that can be described as a society versus nature tension. The order of society is often at odds with both a wildness in people and a wildness in the natural world. Yet people have to live in societies, and Hardy writes compassionately about people caught between the demands of society and the demands of their own natures.

Where do I go from here?

So far I have talked about the standard pattern in Hardy's fiction. In discussing a novel, however, you are primarily concerned with capturing and conveying your sense of the unique and special qualities of that work. The next five chapters of this book illustrate how to explore a text in this way. The five novels considered are those which are generally recognised as Hardy's major works (because of limited space I have had to exclude *The Woodlanders*, which many would argue to be as good as any of the five novels I do discuss). In each chapter I start with ideas about the standard pattern of Hardy's fiction, and then look closely at a handful of passages. This is probably the most important thing to grasp about an actual method of working on the text. Indeed, the whole of this book can be reduced to the simple formula of look at a novel with a clear idea of the tension likely to be at the heart of the work, and then look closely at a few passages. This approach makes sure that your ideas are clear from the outset and forces you to focus on the text itself. There might seem something almost dishonest about just discussing a few scenes from a long novel, but it is the case that such detailed focusing will help you write far better criticism than if you attempt to discuss too much.

As you read the following chapters, do try to remember that I am primarily concerned to illustrate a method of how *you* can work on the text of a Hardy novel. Try selecting and discussing scenes yourself: the moment you do this you should discover how enjoyable and rewarding working on the text on your own can be. It might be the case that you only want to read the chapter about the Hardy novel you are studying, but you could find it useful to read this book as a whole. The reason for saying this is that I cannot cover every aspect of Hardy in every chapter, so it may well be that issues that are central in the novel you are studying are in fact discussed elsewhere. Even if I cannot persuade you to read all the chapters, however, it might be a good idea to read the next chapter, on *Far from the Madding Crowd*, as it is here that I explain most fully the method for working on a text that this book as a whole employs and illustrates.

2

Far from the Madding Crowd

I Constructing an overall analysis

RATHER than offering any introductory comments about *Far from the Madding Crowd*, I will begin straightaway with the method of analysing a novel that I am going to use throughout this book.

(1) After reading the novel, think about the story and what kind of pattern you can see in the text

Bathsheba Everdene inherits her father's farm and takes over as its owner. She is loved by Gabriel Oak, who is just establishing himself as a sheep farmer. When his flock is destroyed in an accident Gabriel finds employment on Bathsheba's farm. Another man in love with Bathsheba is a neighbouring farmer, Boldwood, but Bathsheba loves and marries a soldier, Sergeant Troy, who has deserted Fanny Robin, the mother of his child. After a few months of marriage Troy also deserts Bathsheba, making it appear that he has drowned. Believing she is a widow, Bathsheba accepts a proposal from Boldwood only for Troy to reappear. Boldwood shoots him, is arrested, and confined as criminally insane. The novel ends with Bathsheba marrying Gabriel.

As you start to think about this story bear in mind that novels usually focus on tensions between individuals and society. You might decide to start, therefore, by giving some thought to the society presented and also to the main characters. One thing that you might well conclude from your reading of the novel is that there is little to find fault with about the attractive farming community in which it is set. By contrast, the characters, with the exception of Gabriel, are seen to be controlled by powerful, unruly instincts and to be fairly extreme in their behaviour. Love is at the centre of the story, but it is a love that creates problems. Indeed, in Bathsheba's unwise love for Troy, in Troy's cruel treatment of both Fanny and Bathsheba, and perhaps most clearly in Boldwood's extreme passion that leads him to commit murder, it can be seen that love is presented as an irrational and at times destructive passion which leads people to act in a way that society might well condemn as irresponsible. Hardy, it could be said, is focusing on a reckless instinct in individuals that creates problems within the social order. This might seem a lot to deduce just from the story, but if you think in terms of how novels always present us with a conflict between society and individuals, this should enable you to make rapid progress towards detecting a pattern in any novel.

With a Hardy novel, however, you can make further progress if you also search for a tension between society and nature. Life in this farming community might seem attractive, with men and nature in harmony, but nature can prove wild or simply indifferent to human needs. This is evident in the accident which destroys Gabriel's flock, and in the way a successful harvest is seen to depend upon the luck of good weather; a sudden storm can ruin everything. This potential wildness of nature is similar to the wildness of behaviour of some of the characters. They are members of society but often governed by their natural instincts, and Bathsheba, Troy and Boldwood, as the summary makes clear, all surrender to their instincts.

Can you see what I have done so far? I have tried to get at the issues at the heart of the novel by thinking in terms of society, nature and the individual, and searching for conflicts. Obviously, you should not just accept my overall impression of the work: apply the idea of an opposition to your own summary of the novel, trying to define your own sense of the issues involved.

(2) Select a short passage featuring one of the main characters and try to build upon the ideas you have established so far

Once you have established some sense of an overall pattern you can move on to working out a more detailed view of the novel. The best way to achieve this is to focus on small areas of the text: you will not only be illuminating these particular passages but also gaining a more confident understanding of the novel as a whole. But how do you choose appropriate passages for discussion? A sensible first move is to look at one of the main characters: as this novel starts with Gabriel Oak he seems a suitable choice. Any passage in which he appears could be looked at, but it is a good idea to choose a scene where the character is experiencing some kind of crisis in his or her life or where the dramatic action is tense, as at such points the issues in the novel are likely to be sharply focused.

Just such a passage featuring Gabriel appears early in the novel when he loses his sheep. They have been driven over the edge of a cliff by one of his sheepdogs, and the narrator describes Gabriel's response:

> Oak was an intensely humane man: indeed, his humanity often tore in pieces any politic intentions of his which bordered on strategy, and carried him on as by gravitation. A shadow in his life had always been that his flock ended in mutton – that a day came and found every shepherd an arrant traitor to his defenceless sheep. His first feeling now was one of pity for the untimely fate of these gentle ewes and their unborn lambs.
>
> It was a second to remember another phase of the matter. The sheep were not insured. All the savings of a frugal life had been dispersed at a blow; his hopes of being an independent farmer were laid low – possibly for ever. Gabriel's energies, patience, and industry had been so severely taxed during the years of his life between eighteen and eight-and-twenty, to reach his present stage of progress, that no more seemed to be left in him. He leant down upon a rail, and covered his face with his hands.
>
> Stupors, however, do not last for ever, and Farmer Oak recovered from his. It was as remarkable as it was characteristic that the one sentence he uttered was in thankfulness:
>
> 'Thank God I am not married: what would *she* have done in the poverty now coming upon me!'
>
> [*Far from the Madding Crowd* (New Wessex edition, 1974), p. 73]

You have selected a passage, but what do you say about it? Sometimes you might know exactly what you want to say, but if you are unsure it is a good idea to tackle the passage systematically. Try following this sequence of steps:

(a) A short statement of what the passage is about
(b) Search for an opposition or tension within the passage
(c) Analyse the details of the passage, relating them to the opposition already noted
(d) Try to say how the passage relates to the novel as a whole
(e) Search for anything distinctive about the passage, particularly in the area of style, which you have not already noted

This set of steps underlies the analyses of all the extracts discussed in this book, but it is only in this chapter that I number each step. Of course, you might not always want to work through every step, but setting yourself these tasks should help organise your response.

If we look at the passage above, it is clear that (a) it is about Gabriel's response to the loss of his sheep. (b) The tension I see is between the wildness of nature and the steady, social virtues of

Gabriel. The first paragraph stresses his humanity, his concern for others, and when disaster strikes he only momentarily gives way to self-pity. He almost immediately pulls himself together and thanks God that he is not married. As against the cruel indifference of nature, therefore, we have an impression of a considerate and thoughtful man in Gabriel. (c) The details in the passage help convey this sense of how solid and unselfish Oak is. The narrator tells us that 'Oak was an intensely humane man', and a favourable impression is created by the references to the self-discipline that he has had to maintain to establish himself in the world. The general impression is of a gentle character in a world where everything can be 'dispersed at a blow'. (d) The assumption you have to make in looking at a passage is that it will reflect the larger concerns of the novel. When you look at an extract, therefore, you must step back and relate it to the novel as a whole, trying to sum up what the passage has added to your overall impression. What you might conclude from this passage is that Gabriel seems unlike several of the other characters. Whereas they seem to think only of themselves, Gabriel allows a sense of his social responsibilities to dominate in his thinking and behaviour. This is reflected in his actions throughout the novel: for example, it is Gabriel who almost single-handedly protects the hay-ricks from the approaching storm. He is the embodiment of social virtues in a world where so many of the people and nature itself seem to run wild. (e) The final step in looking at a passage is a close look at its style, but I am going to ignore that for the moment as I want to conclude this section by summing up what you should be trying to do as you turn to the text. It is quite straightforward: you should be trying to flesh out and develop your initial ideas so that you are starting to build a fuller sense of the novel.

(3) Select a second passage for discussion

Each additional passage you consider should add to your overall impression: keep on asking yourself, what can I now say about this novel that I did not know before? The best way to select passages for discussion is to look again at those scenes that have stayed most vividly in your memory, but in this chapter I am going to work through the text mainly on the basis of looking at scenes featuring the main characters. The most striking of these is Bathsheba. A testing moment for her comes when, newly established as a farmer, she makes her first appearance in the cornmarket at Casterbridge:

Two or three only of the farmers were personally known to Bathsheba, and to these she made her way. But if she was to be the practical woman she had intended to show herself, business must be carried on, introductions or none, and she ultimately acquired confidence enough to speak and reply boldly to men merely known to her by hearsay. Bathsheba too had her samplebags, and by degrees adopted the professional pour into the hand – holding up the grains in her narrow palm for inspection, in perfect Casterbridge manner.

Something in the exact arch of her upper unbroken row of teeth, and in the keenly pointed corners of her red mouth when, with parted lips, she somewhat defiantly turned up her face to argue a point with a tall man, suggested there was potentiality enough in that lithe slip of humanity for alarming exploits of sex, and daring enough to carry them out. But her eyes had a softness – invariably a softness – which, had they not been dark, would have seemed mistiness; as they were, it lowered an expression that might have been piercing to simple clearness.   [pp. 123–4]

(a) The passage is about Bathsheba's first appearance in the cornmarket. (b) Various oppositions could be spotted. It could be said, for example, that masculine and feminine are set against each other here. If you took up this idea you could argue that the novel as a whole is largely about how two women, Bathsheba and Fanny, fare in a society where masculine values dominate. The opposition I want to look at, however, is a more direct expression of Hardy's society versus nature tension. Consider the difference between the two paragraphs: the first is largely about the business of the cornmarket, but the second seems mainly concerned to convey a sense of Bathsheba as an unusual personality. It is as if a dynamic, natural presence has surfaced in the well-regulated social world of the cornmarket. (c) This opposition is reflected in the words chosen, with the use of phrases such as 'practical woman' and 'business must be carried on' as Hardy describes Bathsheba feeling her way in this world. Even in the first paragraph, however, Bathsheba seems distanced from conventional conduct: there is a stress on her acting a part as she 'adopted the professional pour'. It is the second paragraph, though, that really stresses how she is at odds with this business world, how she is a defiant, rather tantalising character, with 'something' about her that is difficult to pin down. (d) I now need to pull back and relate these impressions to my ideas about the novel as a whole. I have already talked about a wildness that characterises some people, but one important aspect of this that I have not acknowledged so far is how attractive this can seem in a world of cash values and business deals. (e) Compared to Oak, Bathsheba might seem unreliable and flighty, but if you look at how Hardy writes about her, the impression that comes across is positive rather than negative. The sheer attractiveness of the description, with phrases such as 'that lithe slip of humanity', suggests that Hardy finds her beguiling. In the heavy world of the cornmarket she is light and natural. Yet there is a disturbing side: the idea that she might do 'alarming' things for a woman, that she might refuse to accept a conventional woman's role, suggests that she might create chaos in the society of the novel.

(4) Select a third passage for discussion

I hope it is clear how simple this method of analysis is: all it involves is having a few controlling ideas and then interpreting passages in the light of these ideas. It is a simple method, but it should enable you to produce your own distinctive reading of the novel as you respond to what you think is central in a passage and then relate it to your developing sense of the work as a whole. One of my controlling ideas is the notion of natural instincts that can cause havoc in society. It is an idea which is reflected again in Hardy's presentation of Sergeant Troy, the soldier Bathsheba marries. In this passage he wields his sword around Bathsheba, eventually cutting off a lock of her hair:

> In an instant the atmosphere was transformed to Bathsheba's eyes. Beams of light caught from the low sun's rays, above, around, in front of her, well nigh shut out earth and heaven – all emitted in the marvellous evolutions of Troy's reflecting blade, which seemed everywhere at once, and yet nowhere specially. These circling gleams were accompanied by a keen rush that was almost a whistling – also springing from all sides of her at once. In short, she was enclosed in a firmament of light, and of sharp hisses, resembling a skyfull of meteors close at hand.   [p. 216]

This might seem a very difficult passage to discuss. Even after selecting it I felt tempted to search for something more straightforward, but I decided to stick with it to show how any passage is really quite easy to analyse. As always, the thing to do is to work through a series of steps, starting with the fact that (a) the extract is about Troy wielding his sword around Bathsheba. (b) It seems to me there is a contrast between how things had been a moment before – 'In an instant the atmosphere was transformed' – and how they are now. Things had been safe, but now everything is alarming. (If you find it hard to see an opposition in a passage, it is always worth thinking in terms of a potential tension between conventional life and some activity or attitude that goes against the grain of routine behaviour.) (c) The details of the writing, however, suggest that the experience is not just alarming but also exciting. It is as if, for a moment, Bathsheba is outside common experience and existing in a more dramatic world. It is dangerous, but it is all infused with a dazzling light. (d) The force of this passage is that while it recognises the danger of extreme behaviour it also sees it as glamorous and exciting, and this is consistent with the impression of Troy that comes across in the novel as a whole. He is simultaneously a dangerous and attractive character. We can see why Bathsheba is attracted to Troy rather than Oak: Oak has plenty of virtues but is too steady. Troy, by contrast, is reckless, but it is this very lack of restraint that helps make him attractive. Hardy does not neglect to show us Troy's cruelty or his brutal mistreatment of women, but he remains an alluring figure. (e) The style of the passage tells us why: Hardy uses a great many words such as 'light', 'reflecting' and 'gleams' which convey Troy's glamorous, dazzling quality, yet it would also be an appropriate response to feel that such words also convey a sense of him as flashy and untrustworthy.

(5) Select a fourth passage for discussion

My analysis of the novel so far has centred on the idea of instinctive human behaviour at odds with socially responsible behaviour. I now want to see how Boldwood fits into this scheme of things. I have selected a passage where Boldwood, who does not know that Troy and Bathsheba are already married, is trying to bribe Troy to abandon his interest in her:

> In making this statement Boldwood's voice revealed only too clearly a consciousness of the weakness of his position, his aims, and his method. His manner had lapsed quite from that of the firm and dignified Boldwood of former times; and such a scheme as he had now engaged in he would have condemned as childishly imbecile only a few months ago. We discern a grand force in the lover which he lacks whilst a free man; but there is a breadth of vision in the free man which in the lover we vainly seek.   [p. 258]

(a) The passage is about Boldwood. (b) In particular, it contrasts an idea of his former dignified behaviour and his present behaviour as he finds himself consumed by love. (c) The details in the passage make this clear: an impression of the social man – 'the firm and dignified Boldwood of former times' – is set against an idea of someone who has lost his senses – 'childishly imbecile'. The last sentence of the extract states this directly as the narrator talks about an irrational force that directs the lover's behaviour as opposed to the rational force of the free man. (d) This reflects the way Boldwood behaves in the novel. Until Bathsheba sends him a Valentine card he is a dignified figure, but then he becomes consumed by love for her. His passion becomes more and more obsessive until finally the irrational force is so great that he murders Troy. Yet there is a sense in which the irrational instinct we perceive in Boldwood is only an extension of the irrational instinct that governs so much human conduct in the novel. Boldwood, however, is the most disturbing character in the novel. In order to understand why we need to look at Hardy's style. (e) This passage about Boldwood is characterised by its rather elaborately expressed, ambitious statement about the obsessive nature of the lover. By contrast, when Hardy writes about Bathsheba or Troy he usually associates them with attractive imagery, very often imagery of light. The difference suggests why Boldwood is likely to strike us as a disturbing character, whereas so much of the rest of the novel, even though it deals with such serious matters as the break-up of a marriage, cruelty and death, seems light and fresh. It would seem that Hardy, at this stage of his career, prefers to stress the attractive, exciting nature of his events and characters rather than to dwell on and emphasize the gloomier side of things.

(6) Have I achieved a sufficiently complex sense of the novel?

By this stage, having looked at four passages, you should have pieced together a view of the novel. If you are still puzzled, keep on looking at more passages until you feel that you have worked out a coherent reading. Your ideas might well develop in a very different direction from mine, but this is the whole point about this method of looking at a text, that it allows you, as you move from passage to passage, to systematically develop your own interpretation of the novel. At this stage, however, stop and ask yourself whether you feel you have got to grips with the work. Try to be precise: what still puzzles you about the novel?

One big gap that I am aware of in my analysis of *Far from the Madding Crowd* is that, as I have concentrated on the characters, I have said very little about the setting in which the events take place. The sensible thing to do now, therefore, is to look at a relevant descriptive passage. The one that most appealed to me appears after Bathsheba has slept outside one night after Troy has rejected her. As she awakens in the morning she looks at her surroundings:

From her feet, and between the beautiful yellowing ferns with their feathery arms, the ground sloped downward to a hollow, in which was a species of swamp, clothed with fungi. A morning mist hung over it now – a fulsome yet magnificent silvery veil, full of light from the sun, yet semi-opaque – the hedge behind it being in some measure hidden by the hazy luminousness. Up the sides of this depression grew sheaves of the common rush, and here and there a peculiar species of flag, the blades of which glistened in the emerging sun, like scythes. But the general aspect of the swamp was malignant. From the moist and poisonous coat seemed to be exhaled the essences of evil things in the earth, and in the waters under the earth.   [p. 329]

I must admit that as a student I would not have had a clue what to say about a passage such as this, but any passage can be coped with if you approach it in a systematic way. Part of the secret is telling yourself that the passage must be dealing with issues which you have already registered as central in the novel.

Let us see, then, what can be made of this passage. (a) It is about Bathsheba's surroundings and what she sees when she wakes up in the morning. (b) You might find it hard to spot an opposition here, but bear in mind the idea we have already developed of a force at work in life which is simultaneously attractive and dangerous. What strikes me in this passage is, first, that there is a contrast between the snug spot in which Bathsheba has been sleeping and the swampy hollow just alongside, and, second, that there is a contrast between the attractive appearance of the morning mist and the real nastiness of the swamp. (c) The words chosen emphasise the different aspects very effectively: Bathsheba is surrounded by 'beautiful yellowing ferns', the mist is 'a fulsome yet magnificent silvery veil', but the swamp is 'malignant' and 'poisonous'. In addition, the swamp is associated with cruelty in the description of 'the blades' of the flag appearing 'like scythes'. (d) How all this seems to relate to the novel as a whole is that, whereas so far we have seen how Hardy presents a sense of a disturbing force in people, this passage draws attention to something similar in nature itself. It is a force that is just hidden: Bathsheba appears to be in a cosy spot but the swamp is only inches away, and then one might not see it because of the attractiveness of the deceptive mist. This seems to tie in with how Hardy presents his characters, how often there is something dangerous concealed behind an attractive manner, as is particularly the case with Troy. When we spot this in Hardy's nature descriptions, however, we do perhaps get closer to a sense of what makes him distinctive as a novelist, of how he seems to recognise the powerful ambivalence of the natural world which is both attractive and dangerous. (e) When he writes about nature Hardy's writing seems to become especially rich and evocative. It is as if he can rely upon routine prose to describe the daily business of life, but needs to adopt a more poetic manner to suggest intangible forces. What in particular we can draw attention to in this passage is how the repeated images of light and the sun are set against the dark, intangible evil of the swamp with its 'essences'.

Having looked at this passage I feel I can now sum up the impression that the novel as a whole makes on me. Different readers will interpret the evidence differently, but it seems to me that Hardy is writing about the precariousness of the social order that man has created, how it is threatened by unruly forces in both people and nature. The conventional social order might seem to win the day at the end of the novel, when the steady Gabriel marries Bathsheba, but throughout the novel there is a sense of a wildness in people and nature, which is attractive and exciting and dangerous, and which can never really be brought under control. There is nothing particularly original about this reading of the novel, but criticism does not need to strain after imaginative interpretations. What matters is that, as in this analysis of *Far from the Madding Crowd*, you work closely from the evidence of the text to build a coherent reading of the novel which does honestly reflect your own response to the novel.

II Aspects of the Novel

When you have constructed your overall analysis you might want to look more closely at certain aspects of the novel, at the kind of topics that often feature in examination questions. This is something that I take up in the following chapters. In this chapter, I want to deal with the smaller, but perhaps equally important, problem of how to respond critically to each and every scene, character and detail in a text. The first part of this chapter has already shown you how to do this – it is a case of interpreting every detail in the light of the ideas you have already established – but so many students find it hard to make these connections that it might help if I offer some additional guidance here. The examples are all from *Far from the Madding Crowd*, but similar details and features will be encountered in all of Hardy's novels.

We can start with the problem of **seeing the role of a minor character**, for example Fanny Robin. In fact, Fanny is so central to the plot that she might almost be regarded as a major character: she is the woman Troy is engaged to, whom he abandons for Bathsheba, and who dies in childbirth. The obvious response is to say that she is a sad character, but you need to go beyond this and consider how she fits into the larger scheme of things. As always, the best approach is to select a passage for analysis, such as this brief extract where she has come to see Troy in his barracks:

> 'Is it Sergeant Troy?' said the blurred spot in the snow, tremulously.
>   This person was so much like a mere shade upon the earth, and the other speaker was so much a part of the building, that one would have said the wall was holding a conversation with the snow.
>   'Yes,' came suspiciously from the shadow. 'What girl are you?'
>   'O Frank – don't you know me?' said the spot. 'Your wife, Fanny Robin.'
>   [p. 120]

(a) The passage is about Fanny coming to see Troy. When she says she is his wife this is not literally true: she hopes to be his wife. (b) There is a contrast between the harshness of Troy (and the building in which he lives) and the pathetic quality of Fanny, who (c) in the details of the passage is represented as a kind of insignificant speck in the snow. (d) If we look for a society versus nature tension here, we can see how Fanny craves marriage, how Troy rejects her and how she is left outside in a cruel world of nature. Compared with Troy or Bathsheba, who are rebellious by nature, Fanny is primarily a victim, someone who would love to be an ordinary member of society but who is rejected by the man she loves. The point to appreciate here is that minor characters, such as Fanny, can always be seen in terms of the broader thematic concerns that you have already detected in the novel. Each additional character will provide a fresh slant on the themes and add to the overall complexity of the picture presented. But to get hold of a character you do need to look at a passage, or passages, as this will enable you to move beyond vague impressions and help you define a precise idea of how and where the character fits in. Ask yourself simple questions: ask, as I did with this passage, how society is reflected and how nature is reflected in the extract. Most of the characters you will find are, like Fanny, caught somewhere between the ways of society and the ways of nature.

A whole group of characters in Hardy's novels, **the rustics**, can be looked at in a similar way. It is not enough to say that the rustics are quaint and provide some light relief, they too must reflect the broader concerns of the novel and it is again the case that the best way to crystallise your sense of this is to look closely at a passage, or passages, in which they appear. In the following extract, Joseph Poorgrass, Jan Coggan and Mark Clark are discussing religion. Coggan offers his view:

'I've never changed a single doctrine: I've stuck like a plaster to the old faith I was born in. Yes; there's this to be said for the Church, a man can belong to the Church and bide in his cheerful old inn, and never trouble or worry his mind about doctrines at all. But to be a meetinger, you must go to chapel in all winds and weathers, and make yourself as frantic as a skit. Not but that chapel-members be clever chaps enough in their way. They can lift up beautiful prayers out of their own heads, all about their families and shipwrecks in the newspaper.   [pp. 313–14]

(a) Coggan is talking about religion and (b) draws a contrast between church folk and chapel members. (c) The former do not worry about doctrines, and manage to reconcile their religious faith and their liking for a drink. The chapel members, by contrast, act in an extreme way, going to chapel 'in all winds and weathers'. (d) The passage is likely to strike you primarily as funny, and it might seem very hard to see how it could possibly have any broader significance in the text. But think of the division between society and nature or people's natural instincts that causes so many problems in the book. Someone like Boldwood, for example, cannot reconcile his roles as dignified farmer and passionate lover. By contrast, what Coggan is talking about is a kind of balance in life. Unlike the main characters, the rustics are not extreme in their attitudes or behaviour. In a way they reflect how most people live: they have a humorous view of life which accepts that there are problems but that it is always possible to muddle along on a middle course. They have achieved a working compromise, unlike the main characters who cannot reconcile their social obligations and their natural instincts, and this homely philosophy is expressed in their actions and their speeches. Hardy always presents the rustics in the same way in his novels, but this does not mean that he is holding up their position as an ideal or answer to life's problems, for central to his whole stance as a writer is a recognition that people can be gripped by natural instincts that they cannot control. Perhaps the best way of placing the rustics is to say that their attitude to life helps define the problems experienced by the main characters.

What should be obvious by now is that wherever you turn in a Hardy novel you will encounter some sense of a conflict between social convention and order and a whole range of disruptive instincts and passions. This is equally evident in big dramatic scenes and in the smallest details of a text. To consider **big dramatic scenes** first: in all of Hardy's novels there are vivid scenes of action, scenes which are tremendously visual. Examples in this novel are Troy's sword-play, the hay-rick fire, and the scene where Oak has to battle to protect the gathered corn from an approaching storm. They are often quite long scenes, but in order to analyse them it is sufficient to focus on a couple of paragraphs. As always, try to see how the larger concerns of the novel are reflected and expressed in the extract you are considering. And it should be particularly easy to see this in such scenes, as such dramatic moments tend to throw the concerns of the novel into very sharp focus. If you looked at the hay-rick fire, for example, what you would be likely to conclude is that the dutiful and resourceful Gabriel is battling to contain and control an extreme force. In Hardy's big dramatic scenes, then, you should find the tensions of the novel embodied and expressed in a particularly striking way.

With **small details**, however, you might have to use a little more ingenuity and imagination to see how they relate to the text as a whole. What you can be sure of is that in some way they will reflect the central society versus nature opposition of Hardy's fiction. I will look at just one such detail here. Hardy offers a very full description of how a gargoyle, a water-spout, pours water onto Fanny's grave. One sentence of the description reads, 'The persistent torrent from the gargoyle's jaws directed all its vengeance into the grave.' (p. 341). That is obviously vivid, but if it makes an impact on the reader it must be because there is quite a lot of meaning behind it. The meaning that strikes me is that nature just shows total indifference to, and a lack of respect for, the sanctity of the grave. The point I am making here is that every small detail in the text will, in some way, be reflecting the novel's larger concerns; you might have to niggle away at some details that catch your eye before you can work out their place in the scheme of things, but eventually you should always be able to see how they help create the broader impression the novel offers of what it is like to live in a world where the social order is vulnerable and where natural wildness is always only a step away.

3

The Return of the Native

I Constructing an overall analysis

The Return of the Native is an unusual novel. This is apparent from the beginning: it starts with a lengthy description of Egdon Heath. You might find this off-putting and wonder why Hardy describes the setting at such length. As the novel continues, you might find several of the characters, and the incidents in which they are involved, no less puzzling. It is possible, however, to start sorting out a resonse in exactly the same way as illustrated in the previous chapter. Yet at the end of this analysis you might still feel that you have not come to terms with this strange novel. The reason for this is that an initial analysis is likely to concentrate on characters and themes and might miss any real discussion of the form of the novel. In the second half of this chapter, therefore, I suggest some ways of thinking about the form of *The Return of the Native*, but I start here with ideas about an overall analysis.

(1) After reading the novel, think about the story and what kind of pattern you can see in the text

The Return of the Native takes place on Egdon Heath. Eustacia Vye is in love with Damon Wildeve, a publican, but he marries Thomasin Yeobright. Thomasin's cousin, Clym Yeobright, returns to Egdon Heath from Paris where he has been working as a diamond salesman. He now wishes to serve and teach the people of Egdon. He falls in love with Eustacia and they marry, but the marriage is not a success. Eustacia had hoped that he would return to Paris, thus taking her away from the Heath. Things become worse when Clym's eyesight fails and he becomes a furze-cutter. Eustacia at this point renews her relationship with Wildeve, and also unwittingly contributes to the death of Clym's mother. Clym discovers that Eustacia and Wildeve are lovers. She runs off with Wildeve, but during their flight they are drowned. Thomasin marries Diggory Venn, a reddleman who has always loved her, and Clym becomes an itinerant preacher.

As I have explained in the previous chapters, the way to start making sense of a story is to look for a pattern in the plot. In a Hardy novel you should always be able to find evidence of a society versus nature tension at the heart of the material. I am going to discuss this in a sketchy form here, just to indicate how you could start thinking about this novel. The first thing that might strike you is that Egdon Heath must in some way represent nature: even at the outset it seems reasonable to speculate that the order of society will be set against the untamed wildness of the Heath. The characters who live here are likely to be caught between the pull of society and the pull of nature, including their own natures. Consider Eustacia: she wishes to leave the Heath for Paris, as if she craves the social world, but the main impression of Eustacia that comes across is of a rebellious character who is frustrated by the restraint of marriage and who will not conform and discipline herself. As for Clym, he turns his back on the social world and wants to return to a life close to nature, but when he does so it is in the humble and desperate role of a furze-cutter. What you might spot in the story, then, is a pattern which is consistent with the pattern in much of Hardy's fiction: characters caught between society and nature, including their own natures, and Hardy presenting the human drama of the experiences of characters caught in this dilemma. He is not preaching a lesson, not telling us that the characters should have behaved more cautiously or responsibly, but presenting a vivid picture of what could happen to people

(2) Select a short passage featuring one of the main characters and try to build upon the ideas you have established so far

At this point, as you start to look at how Hardy fills out this pattern, you begin to move from a sense of the standard characteristics of Hardy's fiction to an appreciation of the unique qualities of this novel. As always, it makes sense to start with a look at one of the main characters. Eustacia or Clym are the obvious choices, but you might feel that there is an even more important character in the novel: Egdon Heath. It might not be a person but it is certainly a pervasive presence. The Heath dominates from the very first page:

A Saturday afternoon in November was approaching the time of twilight, and the vast tract of unenclosed wild known as Egdon Heath embrowned itself moment by moment. Overhead the hollow stretch of whitish cloud shutting out the sky was as a tent which had the whole heath for its floor.

.[*The Return of the Native* (New Wessex edition, 1974) p. 33]

Try to remember that I am mainly concerned in this book with illustrating a method of analysing a novel; you should find it more rewarding if, rather than echoing my findings about this passage, you look at another passage for yourself. The problem, though, is that whatever passage about the Heath you select you are likely to find yourself wondering what you can say about it apart from the fact that it is a description of Egdon Heath. The thing to tell yourself when you do not know where to begin is that it is always worth searching for a tension in a passage between some impression of the conventional social order and something that runs counter to the usual social order. If you think about the passage above, there is something untameable about the Heath. The description of it as an 'unenclosed wild' makes it clear that it is not fenced off into fields: here is an area of wildness where society has not imposed its patterns and control. And when Hardy writes that it 'embrowned itself moment by moment', he seems to suggest that the Heath has an active life of its own, that it has an uncontrollable life force. What also strikes me, however, is that it is not a very attractive description of the Heath, as if there is a rather disturbing force at work here, even perhaps a malignant force.

How can these impressions be related to the novel as a whole? Well, I said at the outset that *The Return of the Native* is a strange novel, and part of this must be that it gives such great prominence to a strange force in nature. The whole of the opening chapter is devoted to a description of Egdon, and the effect of this is that it impresses very forcefully on our minds a sense of a force in nature, but a force of a rather disturbing, perhaps inexplicable, kind.

(3) Select a second passage for discussion

A look at Eustacia should prove productive at this point. Any passage in which she appears would tell you a lot about her personality and her role in the novel; the extract I have selected describes her response after a meeting with Wildeve in the early stages of the novel. He leaves her, and the narrator writes:

Eustacia sighed: it was no fragile maiden sigh, but a sigh which shook her like a shiver. Whenever a flash of reason darted like an electric light upon her lover – as it sometimes would – and showed his imperfections she shivered thus. But it was over in a second and she loved on. She knew that he trifled with her; but she loved on. She scattered the half-burnt brands, went indoors immediately, and up to her bedroom without a light.   [p. 92]

The tension I see in this passage is between the idea of the 'flash of reason' Eustacia sometimes experiences and the irrational force of love which seems far more dominant in her personality. It is the kind of tension that could be expected in a Hardy novel: reason, a social virtue, is set against irrational feelings and the result is that we see social attitudes and instinctive feelings at war in a personality. All the details underline this conflict. There seems something extreme about Eustacia: even when she sighs it is not a 'fragile maiden' sigh but a sigh that seems to consume her. A flash of reason, associated here with the domestic idea of 'an electric light', is only a momentary thing for Eustacia. As against this, the phrase 'she loved on' is repeated, the repetition helping to emphasise the instincts which dominate her behaviour. What can also be seen in the passage is use of light and dark imagery: this suggests that there is a daytime world of rational behaviour whereas Eustacia is associated more with the world of darkness and strange forces.

This idea of a dark, strange force in Eustacia clearly ties up with the dark, strange force of Egdon Heath. As in all Hardy's novels, these natural forces and instincts come into conflict with social attitudes and conventions, but what is distinctive about *The Return of the Native* is just how central the undisciplined side of things is. Hardy seems to lean towards a presentation of what is extreme both in the natural setting and in people. This is evident in the extent to which Egdon Heath dominates the novel and in the fact that, although characters in *Far From the Madding Crowd* yield to their instincts, Eustacia seems entirely ruled by her instincts. Yet people have to live with other people, and the drama of the novel is produced by showing how an extremist such as Eustacia fares in the social world: there is initially her fraught relationship with Wildeve, then her fraught relationship with Clym, plus subsidiary strands such as her awkward relationship with Clym's mother.

(4) Select a third passage for discussion

If you have managed to draw some conclusions about Eustacia you might well want to move on to consider Clym. I opened the novel at random and found the following scene between Clym and his mother.

Clym has announced that he hopes to marry Eustacia; his mother replies:

'You are blinded, Clym,' she said warmly. 'It was a bad day for you when you first set eyes on her. And your scheme [*Clym has said that he hopes to start a school*] is merely a castle in the air built on purpose to justify this folly which has seized you, and to salve your conscience on the irrational situation you are in.'

'Mother, that's not true,' he firmly answered.

'Can you maintain that I sit and tell untruths when all I wish to do is to save you from sorrow? For shame, Clym! But it is all through that woman – a hussy!'

Clym reddened like fire and rose. He placed his hand upon his mother's shoulder and said, in a tone which hung strangely between entreaty and command, 'I won't hear it. I may be led to answer you in a way which we shall both regret.'   [p. 216]

It is easy enough to see that Clym and his mother are rowing and that Eustacia is the cause of the disagreement, but the scene needs to be related to the ideas we have been developing. In looking at the previous passage I noted the contrast between rational and irrational behaviour, and here Clym's mother says that he is caught in an 'irrational situation' and is building 'a castle in the air'. The point is that she is asking him to behave as any reasonable and sensible person would, but Clym rejects her advice. He does not wish to offend her but the force of his feeling for Eustacia is greater. Clym, then, like Eustacia, is swayed by his feelings, but, whereas Eustacia seems romantic and passionate, Clym seems more of an idealist and a dreamer. The marriage between these two is a marriage of two people of unconventional, impractical temperaments; Hardy's concern, we can say, then, seems to be with the experiences of people with extraordinary natures in the ordinary situations of life.

(5) Select a fourth passage for discussion

Clym moves away from his mother and begins a relationship with Eustacia. Wildeve marries Thomasin but is still attracted to Eustacia. Mrs Yeobright decides to send some money to Clym and Thomasin, but this falls into the hands of Wildeve. Diggory Venn wins it back off him, however, and by mistake sends all the money to Thomasin, thus unintentionally widening the rift between mother and son. Any or all of these developments could be discussed, but your approach is likely to be most productive if you focus on just one or two small sections. I have decided to look at part of the scene where Wildeve and Venn are gambling:

Wildeve was a nervous and excitable man; and the game was beginning to tell upon his temper. He writhed, fumed, shifted his seat; and the beating of his heart was almost audible. Venn sat with lips impassively closed and eyes reduced to a pair of unimportant twinkles; he scarcely appeared to breathe. He might have been an Arab, or an automaton; he would have been like a red-sandstone statue but for the motion of his arm with the dice-box.   [p. 251]

We can start with Wildeve. The passage tells us that he was 'a nervous and excitable man': as in so much of the novel there is a stress on passionate and irrational feelings in a character. That character is then brought into contact and conflict with other people. This dark force in people seems to have much in common with a dark force in nature itself which is exemplified here in this gambling scene taking place at night, and with the added complication that there seems to be some baffling, mysterious power controlling events. In this area of strange powers, an incident in the novel you might recall is Susan Nunsuch sticking pins into an effigy of Eustacia; Hardy always seems willing to acknowledge that mysterious powers might exist.

But what of Venn? His whole body is red, as a consequence of his job as a reddleman, and he appears very strange as if he is some other-worldly spirit. But if you think about Venn's role in the novel as a whole, his strangeness is all on the surface. Unlike those characters who are motivated by instinct, irrational feelings and undisciplined forces and who find themselves clashing with conventional society, Venn is thoroughly conventional. He wants a happy marriage and a secure job, and in his actions in the novel is anxious to promote general well-being. Venn, then, helps us understand what the novel is about: just as he is strange on the surface yet normal underneath, for the most part in Hardy's world it is the case that beneath the veneer of normality and social convention are all kinds of extreme passions, forces and feelings.

(6) Have I achieved a sufficiently complex sense of the novel?

The thing about characters who will not observe social conventions is that they are likely to come to grief, because if you want to live in society you have to accept the rules of society. What makes the novel interesting, however, is not the abstract exploration of such themes but the fact that it makes abstract themes concrete by dramatising the lives of characters caught in extreme predicaments. For example, throughout the novel we might well sympathise with Eustacia because we know she is bound to be defeated. She cannot settle down and live an ordinary life, and, as much as she might long for a glamorous alternative existence in Paris, there is no escape from the realities of everyday experience except through death. And we see this at the end of the novel where Eustacia and Wildeve, preparing to flee the Heath, die in the weir. The text does not make it clear whether Eustacia falls in or kills herself, but, although this question cannot be answered, a look at the death scene should answer some remaining questions about the novel. I have selected the paragraphs where Wildeve throws himself in:

> Wildeve meanwhile had arrived on the former side, and the light from Yeobright's lamp shed a flecked and agitated radiance across the weir-pool, revealing to the ex-engineer the tumbling courses of the currents from the hatches above. Across this gashed and puckered mirror a dark body was slowly borne by one of the backward currents.
>
> 'Oh, my darling!' exclaimed Wildeve in an agonized voice; and, without showing sufficient presence of mind even to throw off his great-coat, he leaped into the boiling caldron.   [p. 387]

The scene takes place at the weir: a weir is a man-made device set in a waterway in an attempt to control the flow. That seems to sum up much of what the novel is about: there is a natural turbulence, which society attempts to quell and suppress, but that dangerous and voilent power can never really be controlled.

Clym arrives with a light that illuminates Eustacia's 'dark body'. This sustains a pattern of imagery seen throughout the novel: there is a constant tension between the rational, daylight world and the dark world of the night, nature and the mind, and much of the novel is concerned with the meeting of the two. Clym on this occasion is the rational man whereas Wildeve leaps into the 'boiling caldron'. Eustacia, although she might have dreamed of Paris, also seems more at one with the turbulence of nature into which she is now absorbed. By contrast, we see that Clym at the end of the novel is still bizarrely caught between society and nature: he wants to serve his fellow men, but cannot find a conventional role in society and so becomes a rather grotesque misfit.

Or at least, that is the conclusion I draw. Your examination of the evidence might lead you to see things differently. What I do hope is plain by this stage, however, is that the analytic method illustrated here is very simple and straightforward. The controlling principle all the time is to keep to a few ideas, then interpret the details in the light of those ideas, and steadily you should find yourself constructing your own coherent view of the novel.

II Aspects of the Novel

The emphasis of this chapter so far has been on characters and themes in *The Return of the Native*. To discover more, keep on looking at relevant scenes. You might, for example, want to consider Mrs Yeobright, Clym's mother: look at a couple of scenes in which she appears, read them in the light of the ideas you have established, and you should be able to work out your own view of her part in the novel. What you might decide is that of all the characters she is the one who would most like a stable, conventional life. It follows almost inevitably from this that she is the character who is most lost in the natural world of Egdon, and, indeed, she dies on the Heath.

At this point, however, rather than looking directly at characters and themes, you might want to consider some broader issue, for example you might want to think more fully about the strangeness of the novel and **the criticism** frequently levelled against it **that it is exaggerated and improbable**. As in constructing an overall analysis, the best way to organise your thinking on this aspect of the text is to focus on a series of short passages, otherwise you might never get beyond offering an unsubstantiated opinion on whether you find the novel convincing or unconvincing. You have got to take a hard look at the text, showing where and how the writing is strange or exaggerated. You might decide to start by considering Eustacia. As the issue being considered is the strangeness of the novel you need to find a passage, such as this one, where she is described in unusual terms:

> Eustacia Vye was the raw material of a divinity. On Olympus she would have done well with a little preparation. She had the passions and instincts which make a model goddess, that is, those which make not quite a model woman. Had it been possible for the earth and mankind to be entirely in her grasp for a while, had she handled the distaff, the spindle and the shears at her own free will, few in the world would have noticed the change of government. There would be the same inequality of lot, the same heaping up of favours here, of contumely there, the same generosity before justice, the same perpetual dilemmas, the same captious alternation of caresses and blows that we endure now.   [p. 93]

It is easy to see that this is inflated writing, with an odd idea at the centre as Eustacia is discussed as a goddess. If you wanted to find fault with the passage, and by implication with the whole presentation of Eustacia, you could point out that she is just an insignificant young woman living in a remote corner of England and that therefore it is inappropriate to describe her in these terms. You could argue that Hardy is straining too hard to make his novel feel weighty. A more constructive approach, however, would be to try to find a positive reason why Hardy chooses to present Eustacia in these terms.

This should not prove too difficult as you should be able to find an explanation that follows on naturally from the ideas established in your initial analysis. To be more precise, you should be able to construct your answer making use of the idea of a tension between society and nature. Look for a tension in the passage: the one that strikes me is the simple contrast between the world of the gods and the everyday world. The details of the passage spell out how, as a goddess, Eustacia would make no effort to alter the unfairness of existence. If we relate this to the novel as a whole, what we can say is that Hardy is maintaining his idea of how there are forces at work in nature, and, it seems here, in the heavens, which are simply indifferent to mankind's lot. By describing Eustacia in the terms he does, Hardy associates her with an irrational side of existence. The defence of Hardy's way of presenting her is that this is the approach demanded by his theme. Throughout the novel he sets up a conflict between rational social behaviour and a strange but powerful irrational force in nature and people; in order to convince us that there is such a strange quality to Eustacia his writing has to rise to the challenge of conveying something extraordinary about her. When Hardy mentions her 'passions and instincts' it helps enforce the idea of irrational forces surfacing in daily experience, and generally in the novel Eustacia is described as a goddess or queen and associated with cosmic imagery.

Such inflated writing can, however, lose all touch with everyday reality. You have got to decide whether this is the case in this novel. As always, the best way to discipline your answer is to turn again to an extract. You might look at another inflated passage, or you might try to find a passage where Eustacia is described more as a woman than as a goddess. I think the following comes into this category:

In the meantime Eustacia, left alone in her cottage at Alderworth, had become considerably depressed by the posture of affairs. The consequences which might result from Clym's discovery that his mother had been turned from his door that day were likely to be disagreeable, and this was a quality in events which she hated as much as the dreadful.   [p. 317]

Eustacia is beset by worries prompted by the mistreatment of Clym's mother. They are down-to-earth worries written about in a down-to-earth way; the previous passage stressed her indifference to the concerns of daily life, but here she is immersed in all the worries of daily existence and experiencing common emotions. It is again necessary to find a reason why Hardy writes about Eustacia in this way, in particular we have to justify the change of style. The point that strikes me is that if he just presented Eustacia as an almost mythic figure she would be unconvincing. As it is, his change of style can suggest both her extraordinary qualities and how she is unavoidably a member of society. And this is consistent with Hardy's nature versus society tension, his focus on the meeting point between strange forces and the mundane reality of daily life. His interest seems to be in how extraordinary people fare in ordinary life, and, while he recognises extraordinary forces in nature and people, he also recognises that there is no escape from, or alternative to, ordinary life. The point that can be made about Hardy's way of writing about Eustacia, then, is that he does present her in exaggerated terms – but for a purpose, to convey her extraordinary natural qualities – yet he also writes about her as an ordinary member of society.

In considering the exaggerated manner of the novel you might, at this stage, move on from Eustacia to Hardy's conception and presentation of Egdon Heath. Again, focus on a passage. The whole of the first chapter is a description of the Heath, so an appropriate extract should prove easy to find. What should strike you is that the writing is just as unusual as in some of the descriptions of Eustacia. Try, however, to define in what way the writing is unusual, and then try to justify it. I suspect that the conclusion you will arrive at is that the writing suggests all kinds of strange powers at work in life. This is again something that can be explained in terms of a nature versus society opposition, that there are forces in existence that defy rational understanding, and Hardy's writing has to become unusual to describe something so unusual. But if such writing went on for too long it would seem to lose all touch with everyday reality, so again you might want to show how Hardy's real focus is on where nature and society meet. Choose another passage set on the Heath, but this time featuring one or more of the characters – perhaps the scene where Mrs Yeobright comes to call on Clym and Eustacia but cannot gain entry to their house – and the idea should come across forcefully that daily life has to go on whatever larger forces are operating in the background.

What I hope has come across in the last few pages is that the question of exaggeration in *The Return of the Native* is a straightforward issue to consider if you set about investigating it systematically. It is easy to fall into the trap of just offering loose, impressionistic judgments, whereas if you move through a handful of passages you should be able to construct a detailed examination of the topic. What is obviously also important is that you keep your central ideas clear, and this is quite easy to do if you use the idea of a society versus nature tension to help you organise your explanation of everything. The defence of Hardy's method I arrive at, on the basis of looking at just a couple of scenes, is that he exaggerates and writes in a strange way to convey his idea of an irrational force at work in life. He often seems to write from a great height, invoking cosmic imagery, as if he can look down on the social world. At the same time, however, he recognises that people organise their lives according to social rules and conventions, and Hardy can accept and write from this social perspective. At times he might describe Eustacia as a goddess, but he can also write about her as a foolish young woman. By varying his viewpoint Hardy guards against just dealing with strange powers, and produces a work which consistently focuses on the meeting of the irrational and rational, of the extraordinary and ordinary. You could extend an investigation of this question by picking two further scenes, more or less at random, and showing how strange forces and social forces are frequently found together in a scene.

An issue which relates closely to everything said so far is the question of **Hardy's concept of fate**. It is all too easy to get tied up in knots trying to decide whether Hardy did or did not believe in fate, whereas the whole issue can be approached systematically, by means of looking at a few passages, and using the idea of a nature versus society tension to shape your thinking. What is generally meant by 'fate' in the context of Hardy's novels is that, unlike novelists such as Jane Austen and George Eliot, who always think in social and personal terms, he seems to have a notion of a malignant force behind life which always controls things in a cruel way so that individual lives always end in disaster. In *The Return of the Native* there does, at first sight, seem to be a destructive force at work, a destructive force which means that, at the very least, things go wrong and which, at its worst, causes death. When Mrs Yeobright dies, for example, it can seem as if a malignant spirit has decided to kill her. Such general comments about the text, however, lead nowhere; in order to really see how Hardy handles the concept of fate you need to look at relevant passages.

Choose incidents where things go wrong, where the characters experience some misfortune. For example, in this passage that appears after the death of Eustacia, Clym is blaming himself for her death:

> 'I spoke cruel words to her, and she left my house. I did not invite her back till it was too late. It is I who ought to have drowned myself. It would have been a charity to the living had the river overwhelmed me and borne her up. But I cannot die. Those who ought to have lived lie dead; and here am I alive.'   [p. 394]

What strikes me about this is that, although Clym blames himself, the passage also conveys the impression that the events that have happened are beyond his control. There is a very simple sentence structure, as if 'this happened, and then this happened', as if all this was part of a pattern of things which could not be altered. In addition, there is a stress on Clym's powerlessness to change the course of things in 'but I cannot die', which can be placed alongside the way in which he talks about the river as if it has a will of its own to choose who will live or die. So, although Clym blames himself, his speech also suggests a malignant fate that has predetermined these events and which is as rigid in its course as Clym's sentences are in structure. This idea of a hostile fate is consistent with everything we have established about Hardy so far: he acknowledges the presence of mysterious forces in life, and fate is just such a force. What we can add is that his writing always becomes impressive in an unusual way when he writes about such a strange force.

An objection that can be made, however, is that an artist who explains everything in terms of fate is opting for too simple an explanation, an explanation that fails to acknowledge the variety of forces that might be at work in life. Look, though, at how the previous passage continues, as Diggory Venn immediately challenges everything Clym has said:

> 'But you can't charge yourself with crimes in that way,' said Venn. 'You may as well say that the parents be the cause of a murder by the child, for without the parents the child would never have been begot.'   [p. 394]

It must be clear that Venn's whole manner of speaking is very different from Clym's. As against Clym's abrupt sentences, here is a well-reasoned argument. Indeed, he meets Clym's obsessions with rational thought, and that is really the conflict at the heart of the issue: are irrational forces at work or can the whole pattern be explained in rational terms? Venn thinks in terms of families, that is social units, but even more so in terms of free individuals who think for themselves. The point that emerges from this scene, then, is that Hardy might well present an idea of fate at work in his novel, but he is at the same time thoroughly sceptical. As in all the other passages looked at in this chapter, Hardy's real interest is in that area where natural forces and social forces clash. There isn't a message in his work: he isn't saying that fate controls life, but sustaining a tension between the irrational force of nature and rational social forces.

In order to pursue the question of fate in *The Return of the Native*, look at episodes such as the scene where Wildeve and Thomasin's marriage plans are frustrated or the scene where Mrs Yeobright dies. You should find evidence of how fate could be argued to be at work, but you should also find evidence pointing in the opposite direction, evidence of rational scepticism dismissing the supersitition of fate. My liking for Hardy has a lot to do with the feeling that he maintains a certain balance, that, in dramatising a clash between natural and social forces, he does not opt for one side or the other. But you do not have to agree with me: you might feel that he leans towards the view that fate controls life. The important thing, however, is that you should prove your answer from the evidence of the text by looking at passages and showing how they enable you to draw certain conclusions. But in order to do that well you do need to see that the basic issue in Hardy is always a confrontation between the social and the natural, between the rational and the irrational: that framework gives you the clue to interpreting individual passages.

4

The Mayor of Casterbridge

I Constructing an overall analysis

(1) After reading the novel, think about the story and what kind of pattern you can see in the text

The Mayor of Casterbridge is the story of a man who sells his wife. While drunk Michael Henchard sells his wife at a country fair; the next morning he is struck by remorse, gives up drinking and applies himself to a disciplined life, eventually becoming a prosperous corn merchant and mayor of Casterbridge. Henchard, however, has a fiery temperament and most of the book concentrates on how things go wrong for him. His wife returns, with her daughter, after a period of about twenty years and Henchard remarries her. At the same time a young man called Farfrae comes to Casterbridge and Henchard takes him under his wing. Subsequently, however, they become rivals and as Farfrae goes up in the world Henchard goes down. He loses his business to Farfrae, and then suffers the additional blow of discovering that his daughter, Elizabeth Jane, is really the child of the sailor to whom he sold his wife. It is only when Elizabeth Jane marries Farfrae, though, that Henchard feels he has lost everything, and at the end of the novel he leaves the town and dies.

I am going to set about analysing this novel in exactly the same way as described in the previous chapters except that, on this occasion, I am going to pay slightly more attention to Hardy's role as narrator and to the way in which he presents the work. As always, though, I will start with the story. The incident from which the novel springs is Henchard selling his wife, an act which immediately marks him out as a character who disregards the conventional social and moral order. He is drunk when he sells her, but this only underlines the impression of the essential unsteadiness of his nature. The first thing that is evident, then, is the kind of society versus the individual tension which is always central in Hardy's novels: here is a strong character who by nature goes against the ways of society. The rest of the novel presents his life story, emphasising a conflict in his personality: Henchard is torn between a sense of his social duty and the force of his temperament. For twenty-one years he disciplines himself, abstaining from drink, succeeding in business, and rising to the top of the social hierarchy as mayor. Then, however, his world falls apart, partly through accidents of fate, such as his wife returning, but also because of his fiery nature which seems at odds with the social role he has forced himself to play. The conflict I see in the novel, then, is between social discipline and natural indiscipline.

(2) Select a short passage featuring one of the main characters and try to build upon the ideas you have established so far

The obvious person to look at is Henchard. This passage describes his feelings when he wakes up the morning after selling his wife and realises the enormity of his crime:

'Did I tell my name to anybody last night, or didn't I tell my name?' he said to himself; and at last concluded that he did not. His general demeanour was enough to show how he was surprised and nettled that his wife had taken him so literally – as much could be seen in his face, and in the way he nibbled a straw which he pulled from the hedge. He knew that she must have been somewhat excited to do this; moreover, she must have believed that there was some kind of binding force in the transaction. On this latter part he felt almost certain, knowing her freedom from levity of character, and the extreme simplicity of her intellect. There may, too, have been enough recklessness and resentment beneath her ordinary placidity to make her stifle any momentary doubts. On a previous occasion when he had declared during a fuddle that he would dispose of her as he had done, she had replied that she would not hear him say that many times more before it happened, in the resigned tones of a fatalist . . . . 'Yet she knows I am not in my senses when I do that!' he exclaimed. 'Well, I must walk about till I find her . . . Seize her, why didn't she know better than bring me into this disgrace!' he roared out. 'She wasn't queer if I was. 'Tis like Susan to show some idiotic simplicity.'

[*The Mayor of Casterbridge* (New Wessex edition, 1974) pp. 48–9]

A general impression of Henchard as a forceful personality is bound to have come across in your initial reading of *The Mayor of Casterbridge*, but a look at a passage such as this should enable you to talk about him with confidence. What can be seen in the passage is that, on the one hand, Henchard is worried about his behaviour and the social guilt involved – he worries about whether he told anyone his name, presumably in case he is recognised – but, on the other hand, a very selfish side of his personality is also revealed: he is 'surprised and nettled' at his wife, blaming her for what has taken place. He is caught between his social conscience and his instinctive selfishness.

As the passage continues, Henchard speaks: the anger of his speech conveys his explosive temperament, but he is aware of society's rules and standards and can see the disgrace of having acted in such a manner. If we relate these impressions to the novel as a whole, we should be able to see that Hardy is focusing on an undisciplined force in the human character. Presumably the novel is going to raise questions about whether the demands of society and natural instincts can ever be reconciled. This impression is reinforced by the picture we are given of Susan in that the passage suggests that there is also a division in her personality: she always appeared meek, but 'recklessness and resentment' lay beneath her 'ordinary placidity'. There are, it seems, instincts that rebel against conformity even in such a character as Susan Henchard.

Just one more thing: Hardy's stance as narrator. Commenting on how Henchard appeared surprised and nettled, the narrator says that this could be determined from his face and the way in which he nibbled a straw. What strikes me about this detail, and in the passage as a whole, is that Hardy does not convey a moral judgement. Rather than writing from a social viewpoint, it is more as if he is an observer, slightly at a distance from the character and from conventional social attitudes. He is more interested in conveying the picture than in passing judgement, and this, I think, affects our response to Henchard. We can see that, by any conventional standard, he has behaved, and is continuing to behave, deplorably. But as we see him here, irritably nibbling at a straw, a strong connection is established between Henchard and a natural image which can help suggest that it might be the most natural thing in the world to flout society's rules and think only of oneself.

(3) Select a second passage for discussion

So far in this book I have tended to select passages about principal characters. The reason for this is that discussion of characters provides the easiest way into a novel. The concerns of a novel are, however, made clear in every paragraph of that work, and often it is more rewarding and revealing to look at descriptive passages in the text rather than to limit your attention just to character. Hardy's

novels are particularly rich in descriptions, such as this impression of
the congestion in Casterbridge on market day:

> Every shop pitched out half its contents upon trestles and boxes on the kerb,
> extending the display each week a little further and further into the roadway, despite
> the expostulations of the two feeble old constables, until there remained but a
> tortuous defile for carriages down the centre of the street, which afforded fine
> opportunities for skill with the reins. Over the pavement on the sunny side of the way
> hung shopblinds so constructed as to give the passenger's hat a smart buffet off his
> head, as from the unseen hands of Cranstoun's Goblin Page, celebrated in romantic
> lore.
>
> Horses for sale were tied in rows, their forelegs on the pavement, their hind legs in
> the street, in which position they occasionally nipped little boys by the shoulder who
> were passing to school. And any inviting recess in front of a house was utilized by
> pig-dealers as a pen for their stock.   [p. 91]

The first thing that we can say about this passage is that it obviously
adds a great deal of colour to the novel, but the point to grasp about
such passages is that they are not mere description for its own sake but
reflect the broader issues of the text. Here, for example, my
impression is that the town can barely contain the market, that there
is so much activity that the town is almost bursting at the seams. In
turn this perhaps affects how we feel about Henchard, but this is a
point I will turn to in a moment.

First, let us look at how Hardy presents his picture of market day in
Casterbridge. The most striking image, I think, is that of the horses
'tied in rows': their natural energy is thwarted and they act violently
as a result, attempting to bite the passing schoolboys. Hardy goes into
some detail about the way in which they are tied up with 'their
forelegs on the pavement, their hind legs in the street.' The effect of
such details is to suggest that there is something unnatural and
distorted about trying to tie animals down in this kind of way. Yet we
do not only find this natural energy in the horses: everywhere in the
description there is a sense of an energy and life that cannot be
contained. Everything seems close to chaos, with just two pathetic old
constables trying to maintain some kind of order.

The passage suggests, then, both that there is something cramped
about society and also that there is a tremendous natural energy that
the town can barely contain. This idea, that there are forces at work
which can disrupt the peaceful order of life in society, is hinted at
again in the reference to 'Cranstoun's Goblin Page', with its
suggestion of a malign power outside man's control. Taken together,
such details perhaps influence how we think about Henchard. The

previous passage I looked at leant towards a presentation of him as unpleasantly selfish. This passage, however, focuses on the more general idea of unruly forces in life and suggests that Henchard's rebelliousness itself may be a natural, instinctive reaction, that society is too confining for his impulses. The problem he faces, however, and the problem at the heart of the novel, is that he has to live in society.

(4) Select a third passage for discussion

Wherever you look in the novel you should find a tension between social discipline and natural instincts. If you were to consider Farfrae, for example, you might decide to look at a passage from near the beginning of the novel where he sings a sentimental song about his homeland in Scotland. From this you might decide that he is a cold character who confines all his emotional feelings to a sentimental song, yet later in the novel, when he falls in love with Lucetta, he is consumed by love in a totally irrational way. The way to grasp the nature and significance of Farfrae, or indeed any character or any scene in the text, then, is to employ your ideas about a simple tension in the novel. Look at the character or scene searching for the ways in which it is built upon this tension. Don't worry if this tension seems obvious: what really matters in criticism, and what will really bring your sense of the novel to life, is the way in which you develop your analyses of passages in the light of your central ideas. Remember that every scene and any scene will repay analysis. Here, for example, are a couple of paragraphs from an episode where Henchard miscalculates the weather and sells his corn at a loss. Hardy starts by describing the change in the weather:

The fact was, that no sooner had the sickles begun to play than the atmosphere suddenly felt as if cress would grow in it without any nourishment. It rubbed people's cheeks like damp flannel when they walked abroad. There was a gusty, high, warm wind; isolated raindrops starred the window-panes at remote distances: the sunlight would flap out like a quickly opened fan, throw the pattern of the window upon the floor of the room in a milky, colourless shine, and withdraw as suddenly as it had appeared.

From that day and hour it was clear that there was not to be so successful an ingathering after all. If Henchard had only waited long enough he might have avoided loss though he had not made a profit. But the momentum of his character knew no patience. At this turn of the scales he remained silent. The movement of his mind seemed to tend to the thought that some power was working against him.

[p. 215]

By this stage of the novel Henchard is on the way down. For years he has managed to control his natural impulses, directing his energy into building up a business, but now his business and his personal life are beginning to collapse. This passage deals with three factors that disrupt his life and perhaps life generally. One is the weather: there is an unpredictability about nature that shows no respect or concern for man's efforts to gather in a good harvest. Another problem is Henchard's temperament: he is impatient and, surrendering to a sudden impulse, sells. Henchard himself, however, suspects that some malignant force in the universe, a force of fate, might be working against him. In several ways, therefore, the passage presents an idea of undisciplined forces that come in conflict with any attempt to order and direct life.

This passage, therefore, as with every passage in the novel, is expressing and exploring the larger themes of the work. What will also be true of any passage, however, is that it will also tell you a good deal about Hardy's stance as narrator in the novel. If you look at this passage, for example, it might strike you that the second paragraph is written in a no-nonsense style with Hardy offering confident social judgements on Henchard's behaviour. The first paragraph, however, is very different: it could loosely be called poetic, although a more accurate way of putting this is to say that Hardy makes use of a great deal of metaphor and imagery to convey what he is saying. This is appropriate as Hardy here is describing an irrational force in nature that can hardly be defined in a crisp, no-nonsense language. Throughout the novel Hardy moves between these two modes of narration: at times he expresses the judgements that any member of society would make, but at other times he offers an alternative, non-social perspective. What this means is that Hardy is not a moralising narrator. By ordinary standards Henchard is an irresponsible man but viewed from another angle his behaviour is quite natural. A question that might have occurred to you on reading the novel is the question of what explanation of Henchard's downfall does Hardy seem to favour. Does he regard Henchard's personality as the real problem? To take this view, however, is to judge events from a conventional social stance. Hardy does not seem to offer us a single viewpoint in this kind of way. On the contrary, his method seems to be, here is the story of this man's life, what you make of it depends upon your angle of looking. Hardy himself gives us different, even conflicting, views of events and characters, so that we gain a full sense of every implication of his theme of people caught between the

demand of society and the demands of their own, and nature's
impulses.

(5) Select a fourth passage

As the novel enters the final stage Henchard virtually loses his social
identity. His business collapses, he discovers that he is not Elizabeth
Jane's father, he is snubbed by the community, and his guilty past is
revealed. He is pushed and pushes himself into a position of isolation,
but man cannot live in isolation. At the end, therefore, there is no
option for him other than death. The scene I have decided to look at
here presents Henchard provocatively separating himself off from his
fellow men: it is the scene that takes place on the day that he starts
drinking again. For twenty-one years he has held himself in check, but
now he yields to his nature. The scene takes place on a Sunday after
church when the men of Casterbridge adjourn to the pub. The
obvious way to tackle the scene would be to look at the part where
Henchard breaks up their meeting; but the earlier chapters of this
book have already illustrated how you can handle this kind of direct
discussion of character in conflict with society. These earlier chapters
should also help you see how characters such as Elizabeth Jane,
Farfrae and Lucetta can all be compared and contrasted with
Henchard, and how each character exhibits a different balance
between social ambitions and emotional instincts in his or her
personality.

Instead of concentrating directly on Henchard's character, then, I
want to focus, as in the last discussion, on Hardy's manner as
narrator, and for this purpose his general description of
Casterbridge's Sunday ritual tells us all we need to know:

> The great point, the point of honour, on these sacred occasions was for each man to
> strictly limit himself to half-a-pint of liquor. This scrupulosity was so well understood
> by the landlord that the whole company was served in cups of that measure. They
> were all exactly alike – straight-sided, with two leafless lime-trees done in eel-brown
> on the sides – one towards the drinker's lips, the other confronting his comrade. To
> wonder how many of these cups the landlord possessed altogether was a favourite
> exercise of children in the marvellous. Forty at least might have been seen at these
> times in the large room, forming a ring round the margin of the great sixteen-legged
> oak table, like the monolithic circle of Stonehenge in its pristine days.   [p. 255]

The passage is about a long-established, well-regulated tradition
which is part of the stable social fabric of this community. What

strikes me about this gathering is a sense of strain that underlies its order: everything seems strict, sacred and scrupulous as if natural impulses are being excluded. Even the trees represented on the beer-mugs are leafless. And yet, throughout the passage, and as is so often the case in this novel, there are all kinds of hints that life cannot be regulated and contained in this kind of way. There are the children and their interest in the 'marvellous', but most of all there is the reference to Stonehenge. Stonehenge suggests an idea of powerful harmony between mankind and nature that might have existed in the past, when mankind acknowledged and perhaps even worshipped strange powers. But it is a reference that operates at the expense of this prim little circle of men drinking their half-pints. I see this passage, then, as one that again points to the cramped nature of society, and how it excludes and denies the natural energy of life. The problem, however, is that this natural energy is both disruptive and destructive, as Henchard's behaviour in this scene and throughout the novel reveals. In the end, Hardy seems to suggest that the tension between nature and society, between Henchard's fiery temperament and the ways of society, cannot be resolved. And because Henchard cannot come to an accommodation with society no option is open to him other than isolation and death.

(6) Have I achieved a sufficiently complex sense of the novel?

I am aware of much that I have missed out in this analysis of *The Mayor of Casterbridge*. I have concentrated on Hardy's approach as a narrator, and have therefore not said very much about the characters in the novel. I hope, however, that you can see how to tackle issues of content and character in the novel by applying the kind of approach that I have described in the earlier chapters: your focus would most probably be on how various characters either fit in with or find themselves at odds with the community and social convention. You might find some further ideas about this in chapter seven of this book, the chapter about essay writing, where I use a question about the characters in *The Mayor of Casterbridge* as the basis of the discussion.

  For the moment, however, let me try to sum up the main points about Hardy's narrative method that have emerged in this analysis. All of these points are just as significant in relation to his other novels as they are to *The Mayor of Casterbridge*. The first point is that, to a very great extent, Hardy is a visual novelist. He paints the scene, and we, as readers, are asked to interpret what we see. This is one of the things that makes him something other than a moralising narrator. What is also important in this respect is the way in which style varies, the way in which he can switch from a social viewpoint to a far more poetic style that suggests an alternative perspective upon experience. Central in these more poetic passages is Hardy's use of a great deal of natural imagery, which helps to bring to life his theme of nature at odds with society. All of these features of Hardy's manner of writing are attractive and appealing, but perhaps the most important feature of his method for those of us trying to write about his novels is the way in which his details imply so much. In any passage we are likely to encounter social images and natural images, and always the suggestion is likely to be that society is cramped and artificial whereas nature is unrestrained and at times dangerous. But what is perhaps most distinctive about Hardy's style is the way in which the small details he employs constantly imply all the larger concerns of the novel and point off in all kinds of directions. In that last passage we looked at, for example, suddenly to bring in Stonehenge at the end is a marvellously inventive way of raising again the larger concerns of the novel. And this is characteristic of Hardy, both in his novels and in his poetry, that he repeatedly uses telling images that reflect and comment on the fundamental dilemmas of human experience. This holds good whether we approach his novels as tragedies or as novels of social change, as should become clear in the section that follows.

II Aspects of the Novel

Several of Hardy's novels can be regarded as **tragedies**. In order to appreciate this, we first need to understand what a tragedy is. Tragedy is essentially a theatrical form and is the most ambitious form of drama. What happens initially in a tragedy is that the established pattern of life is thrown into disarray: an event takes place early in the work that disrupts the established order of society. The result is that, for the tragic hero in particular, everything falls apart: the hero experiences the collapse of the social order but seemingly of the whole civilised order of society and the collapse of the family order of which he has been a part. Stripped of the protection of family and friends, he, or of course she, has to confront unpleasant facts about life, including unpleasant facts about his or her own nature. In this sense the tragic hero is a specially chosen person who confronts the viciousness that could be said to exist in life. The hero learns so much about the world and mankind that he cannot find a way back into society and has to die. Tragedy might seem a negative form, in that it places so much emphasis on the disorder of life, but what makes tragedy very positive is the sense it conveys of the fortitude of the tragic hero in facing up to the worst of experience.

In some ways the novel form and tragedy seem at odds with each other. This is because the novel is primarily a social form examining the relations between individuals and society. Tragedy is a more extreme form, confronting the entire potential chaos of existence. In a novel we generally receive a clear picture of an actual society, but if you are familiar with any of Shakespeare's tragedies you will know that they are not socially detailed in the same way, that they seem to confront large issues rather than explaining things in terms of social factors and individual psychology. Hardy, as a writer of tragic novels, is thus doing something unusual in the novel form, yet it is easy to understand why he writes tragic novels. We can return to our central society versus nature tension. Whereas the novel is generally a social form, tragedy looks at the whole of the natural world including the extreme facts about human nature. It follows, therefore, that Hardy with his readiness to acknowledge irrational forces in life, is likely to be attracted to a form such as tragedy that permits and encourages an exploration of non-social instincts.

If you want to discuss *The Mayor of Casterbridge* as a tragedy, your best approach as always is to think about the story in the novel, and then focus closely on a few passages. In thinking about the story as a whole, you need to look for the tragic hero and some kind of tragic pattern in the text. Henchard is, of course, the tragic hero: he is a larger-than-life character who, as is always the case with tragic heroes, has a flaw, which in his case is his hot-headed, selfish nature. The established order of society is originally upset by the sale of his wife; after this Henchard carves out a secure life, but then his wife returns and Farfrae arrives, and from that point on things begin to fall apart. As always with a tragic hero, the problems are in part of his own making, that Henchard will not compromise in the way most people would, and as a result he experiences the collapse of the social and family order he has known. He thinks about the universe in which he lives, seeing it as malignant and destructive, bent on his ruin, but he also has to consider a malignancy and destructiveness in his own temperament. After experiencing so much there is no path of return and Henchard inevitably dies.

Very quickly, then, you could show that there is a tragic pattern in the novel, but the plots of many novels could be manipulated in the retelling to make them sound like tragedies. What you need to show is that Hardy is consciously writing a tragedy, that he is attempting to give his material the weight and profundity we associate with tragedy, and the way to do this is to concentrate on specific passages. You might start by looking at a scene from early in the novel – such as the scene where Henchard sells his wife – where some of the personality traits of the hero, including his flawed character, are established. Then, after this, turn to a scene where the hero is beginning to experience some of the blows that life can offer. I have selected the episode where Henchard tells Elizabeth Jane that he is her father and then almost immediately discovers that she is Newson's daughter. Hardy describes his response:

> Misery taught him nothing more than defiant endurance of it. His wife was dead, and the first impulse for revenge died with the thought that she was beyond him. He looked out at the night as at a fiend. Henchard, like all his kind, was superstitious, and he could not help thinking that the concatenation of events this evening had produced was the scheme of some sinister intelligence bent on punishing him.
>
> [p. 154]

There are two things to comment on here: what is happening and the texture of the writing. In terms of what is happening, it can be seen that the tragedy is developing as the whole family order falls apart and Henchard confronts what he feels is a cruel universe. But look as well at the quality of the writing, the way in which Hardy clusters words such as misery, death and revenge in a few lines. The force of such writing is that it encourages us to look beyond the domestic situation presented, it encourages us to think about the larger patterns of life and death. The sheer weightiness of the vocabulary, with words such as 'concatenation', reflects the ambitious scope of the passage, something which is also apparent in the speed with which the sentences move to showing Henchard speculating on some 'sinister intelligence' in life. The whole time Hardy is looking beyond the events themselves and asking questions about the whole cosmic order of things. The point I am making here is that, in discussing *The Mayor of Casterbridge* as a tragedy, you have to show how the text is raising the questions that tragedy usually raises, questions about whether there is any order, meaning or justice in life, questions about the plight of man in the world. You have to prove that Hardy is deliberately giving his novel a certain tragic weightiness. What will help is if you comment on the language he uses, which will be rather heavy but impressive sounding; in addition, try to grasp the nature of the situation presented, seeing how it is one man standing against the universe, confronting the dark powers as if engaged in some heroic struggle for survival.

You will need to look at two or more passages from the central stages of the novel to accumulate your evidence that the novel is indeed working in this way, but then look at Henchard in the latter stages of the novel:

> He experienced only the bitterness of a man who finds, in looking back upon an ambitious course, that what he has sacrificed in sentiment was worth as much as what he has gained in substance; but the super-added bitterness of seeing his very recantation nullified. He had been sorry for all this long ago, but his attempts to replace ambition by love had been as fully foiled as his ambition itself. His wronged wife had foiled them by a fraud so grandly simple as to be almost a virtue. It was an odd sequence that out of all this tampering with social law came that flower of Nature, Elizabeth. Part of his wish to wash his hands of life arose from his perception of its contrarious inconsistencies – of Nature's jaunty readiness to support unorthodox social principles.   [p. 339]

When looking at a passage from late in the work you again need to show how the writing is self-consciously 'tragic', but you also need to see whether the person, who at the outset was seen to have tragic potential, is acting in a suitably heroic manner in the face of the worst that life has to offer. To consider Hardy's style first, some of the writing here is so inflated that I find it hard to understand what he means, but I can see that this heavy and abstract language is being used to ask fundamental questions about life. In particular, we see Henchard confronting the contradictions of his own life and the anomalies and paradoxes of existence. One reason why he is ready to part from life is that there no longer seems any logic to anything.

Henchard, then, does strike us as a tragic hero both here and throughout the novel. Something else reinforces this impression. Very often in tragedy the hero gains a moment or moments of insight at the end when everything seems to make sense to him: in this passage Hardy mentions Henchard's 'perception' of life's 'contrarious inconsistencies'. Such moments in tragedy have considerable intellectual force but their emotional force is also important. Here, we gain a sense of Henchard as a man who has experienced a great deal, who moves between extremes of bitterness and love; as a man who is tired and defeated, but also simultaneously a sense of a man who is heroic in the face of suffering. That is, our impressions of Henchard in this passage are both complex and moving, as befits a tragedy.

You might need to look at another scene from the end of the novel to consolidate your impression, but by now the overall approach should be clear. Start with the story as a whole; then look at the early presentation of the tragic hero; next, look at the situation as it develops and how Hardy writes about it; finally look at the actions and words of the tragic hero to establish your sense of his heroism in the face of adversity. And really the whole question of Hardy as a tragic novelist can be handled as straightforwardly as that. Apart, that is, from one complication.

Although Hardy's novels can accurately be labelled tragedies, this does not seem to sum up the total impression the works make. With Henchard, for example, you might feel that he is a striking and extraordinary hero yet not be able to abandon the feeling that, viewed in any kind of realistic terms, his behaviour is foolish and irresponsible. Similarly, you might feel that Hardy is encouraging you to regard Eustacia in *The Return of the Native* as a tragic heroine, but you might also feel that she is naive and silly. Possibly the novels are encouraging us to take both views. Certainly this seems to fit in with Hardy's double viewpoint as narrator and with the overall tension in his novels between society and nature. Hardy, we have seen, rejects the idea of making sense of life exclusively in social terms: conventional explanations, he seems to imply, do not seem to account for all the facts. He therefore adopts an alternative stance, which in part finds expression in his use of tragedy, a form of writing which allows him to speculate comprehensively on the forces and powers that shape life. But Hardy recognises that people live in societies and that society's views and perspective cannot be dismissed or ignored. Consequently, throughout the novels he seems to adopt a double perspective on things: there is a strong tragic viewpoint in the text, but also a social perspective. At the heart of Hardy's work, then, there is not only a tension between the ways of society and the ways of nature, but this tension is consistently reproduced in the way that he takes both a social and non-social view of events, a tragic and non-tragic view of them.

Where this issue might come up as if you were asked to consider how appropriate it is to describe *The Mayor of Casterbridge* as a tragedy. Can you see how such a question implies that the label tragedy somehow does not describe the total experience of the work? To answer such a question, I would first show the ways in which the novel was a tragedy, using close analysis of specific passages as outlined above, but then, in the last third of my answer, change . direction, trying to show how signals other than tragic signals are coming from the text, I would look for down-to-earth scenes where there was an absence of metaphysical questions about the nature of life. In *The Mayor of Casterbridge* it would not be too difficult to find scenes involving Henchard which suggest something other than a tragic story unfolding, scenes which present a picture of a very detailed and convincing social drama. Henchard might have the grandeur of a tragic hero, but he is also a man who suffers from social problems such as drink, and the collapse of his marriage and business. The reason the text strikes us in this way is that Hardy can switch from one style of narration, which is abstract and speculative, to another style which looks at the events from a conventional social perspective. Writing in such a way adds to the complexity and fullness of his novels, making us aware of the richness of life and its ambivalence rather than of any simple pattern that can be seen in it.

This discussion of Hardy as a tragic novelist has ended up by returning to the one point that you really need to grasp in order to do full justice to the complexity of Hardy's achievement as a novelist. This is that there is always a double view of things in Hardy's novels. An awareness of this double perspective of Hardy's should help you come to terms with any problem or issue in his works, including the important question of **social change** in this novel. Some critics see *The Mayor of Casterbridge* not so much as a tragedy or as a character portrayal of Henchard, but as a novel about a change in the social order in Victorian England in which an old rural economy is yielding to a more calculating view of life. In such a reading Henchard stands as a representative of the old way of doing things, while Farfrae, who is altogether more calculating, and ready to introduce new machinery, stands for everything new.

In order to discuss *The Mayor of Casterbridge* as a social novel, start, as always, by thinking about the story as a whole, trying to see how it could be seen as a novel about the defeat of an old social order and the arrival of a new kind of man with new attitudes. Then, look at a number of scenes: the kind of scenes you might particularly want to consider are those where Farfrae is seen in contention with Henchard, or scenes where there is direct evidence of a new way of life being introduced. One scene that might well capture your attention is when Farfrae introduces a mechanical horse-drill:

It was the new-fashioned agricultural implement called a horse-drill, till then unknown, in its modern shape, in this part of the country, where the venerable seed-lip was still used for sowing as in the days of the Heptarchy. Its arrival created about as much sensation in the corn-market as a flying machine would create at Charing Cross. The farmers crowded round it, women drew near it, children crept under and into it. The machine was painted in bright hues of green, yellow, and reds, and it resembled as a whole a compound of hornet, grasshopper, and shrimp, magnified enormously. Or it might have been likened to an upright musical instrument with the front gone. That was how it struck Lucetta. 'Why, it is a sort of agricultural piano,' she said.   [p. 193]

Your first response to this passage might well be that Hardy introduces the horse-drill as a symbol of the modern world that has arrived in this sleepy town, and which marks another step in the break-up of the old order. Certainly there is a good deal of evidence to support this in the text as the narrator contrasts the 'modern shape' of the drill with the 'venerable seed-lip'. But what you might also spot is the way the new horse-drill is described. Lucetta, struggling to make sense of it, compares it to a piano, the narrator to a mixture of hornet, grasshopper and shrimp. In other words the drill is seen in terms of both natural and social images, reminding us of the basic conflict of the novel as a whole, a conflict which is, in a sense, unchanged by the new horse-drill. It is as if Hardy at once acknowledges the idea of social change but also suggests that this change is only part of a continuing struggle between society and nature in the history of man.

Is, then, *The Mayor of Casterbridge* a novel about change in the rural life of England? That is really for you to decide. As suggested throughout this book, select relevant scenes and comment on what you see in these scenes. It might well be that the overwhelming impression that comes across to you is that Hardy's theme is social change. And if you can actually use the evidence of the text to substantiate that view, then nobody can find fault with your response. What I am suggesting, though, is that a close look at the evidence might well lead you to conclude that Hardy does not interpret the events from just one angle, nor does he allow one view to dominate. Take the encounters between Farfrae and Henchard: if you look closely at one or more of these scenes, the evidence of Hardy's writing might well suggest that his theme is the clash of old and new, but the same scenes can also suggest that it is a clash between two men of different temperaments, and certain qualities in the writing might also suggest that it is fate that has brought these two men into collision. The point is that Hardy does not narrate from just one angle but acknowledges the variety of social, psychological, natural, and even inexplicable forces at work in any event. This might seem a difficult idea to handle, but if you make a point of always working from the evidence of the words on the page you should find that removes many of the problems associated with disciplining and organising your response.

The suggestion that Hardy has no single stance might make him seem an elusive and difficult novelist. What always comes across very forcefully, however, is his sympathy for the individuals caught in the middle, caught between the laws of society and the laws of nature. It is this sense of a vulnerable individual, caught between society and nature, that is central in the next novel we look at, *Tess of the D'Urbervilles.*

5

Tess of the D'Urbervilles

I Constructing an overall analysis

Tess of the D'Urbervilles is in some ways an easy novel to understand. This is because it tells a straightforward story and tells it with great force. Tess, a poor country girl, is raped and made pregnant by Alec D'Urberville. The baby dies and Tess goes to work on a farm. There she meets and marries Angel Clare, but when she tells him about her past he rejects her and goes off to Brazil. Tess then meets Alec D'Urberville again and for a variety of reasons, including the fact that he has persuaded her that Angel will never return, she agrees to live with him. Angel does return, however, and Tess murders Alec. She experiences a few days freedom in company with Angel, but at the end of the novel she is arrested at Stonehenge and subsequently executed. Something of the force of the novel is conveyed in its subtitle 'A Pure Woman': the innocent Tess could be said to be a victim of society's attitudes towards sex and women. What comes across vividly in the novel is Hardy's anger at the way the world treats Tess and his intense sympathy for her. These are feelings that most readers of the novel share: you are likely to find yourself totally on the side of Tess and indignant with Alec and Angel.

It might, however, seem hard to find much else to say about the novel as it can seem such a simple story with such obvious significance. Yet it is a complex novel, and where the complexity lies is in Hardy's telling of the story: he takes a traditional tale of a woman's sufferings, but in his retelling of this old story creates something powerful and original. The way to grasp this, the way to see what Hardy adds to this basic story, is to look closely at a number of passages, but as always your first move should be a consideration of the story as a whole.

*(1) After reading the novel, think about the story and what kind of pattern
you can see in the text*

I have already put together my summary of the novel and made a
suggestion about the kind of society versus the individual tension you
might spot; how Hardy could be said to be presenting a cruel and
inflexible society which victimises and mistreats Tess. If you wanted
to look for a society versus nature and tension in the novel you might
start by considering Tess's feelings for Angel and Angel's feelings for
Tess; what emerges is a conflict between the natural love they feel for
each other and those social attitudes which, in Angel's eyes, make
Tess a fallen woman. Angel's social prejudices are stronger than his
natural feelings. At the heart of the novel, therefore, there is a conflict
between instinctive behaviour and the social dictates which restrict
behaviour.

*(2) Select a short passage featuring one of the main characters and try to
build upon the ideas you have established so far*

What you are really interested in, in any novel, is how the novelist
brings his themes to life. Of central importance in this novel is
Hardy's presentation of Tess. Any passage featuring Tess will tell you
a lot about her, and in the process add to your understanding of the
novel's themes. Here, for example, is a scene from early in the novel
when Tess is walking with the other village girls in a country custom
called 'club walking'. They see Tess's father and the other girls begin
to joke about him being drunk:

'Look here; I won't walk another inch with you, if you say any jokes about him!' Tess
cried, and the colour upon her cheeks spread over her face and neck. In a moment her
eyes grew moist, and her glance drooped to the ground. Perceiving that they had
really pained her they said no more, and order again prevailed.
    Tess Durbeyfield at this time of her life was a mere vessel of emotion untinctured
by experience. The dialect was on her tongue to some extent, despite the village
school: the characteristic intonation of that dialect for this district being the voicing
approximately rendered by the syllable UR, probably as rich an utterance as any to
be found in human speech. The pouted-up deep red mouth to which this syllable was
native had hardly as yet settled into its definite shape, and her lower lip had a way of
thrusting the middle of her top one upward, when they closed together after a word.
    Phrases of her childhood lurked in her aspect still. As she walked along today, for
all her bouncing handsome womanliness, you could sometimes see her twelfth year in
her cheeks, or her ninth sparkling from her eyes; and even her fifth would flit over the
curves of her mouth now and then.
                    [*Tess of the D'Urbervilles* (New Wessex edition, 1974) pp. 42–3]

In Hardy's novels there is frequently a tension between socially correct behaviour and wayward behaviour. This is present here in the idea of Tess's father getting drunk and making a spectacle of himself. Can you see how a similar tension is implicit in Hardy's reference to how Tess would have been taught to speak at the village school? She would have been forced to speak in a 'correct' way, and Hardy contrasts this with her natural dialect: by the standard of the school the local dialect would appear uncouth, but Hardy stresses the richness of these natural sounds. In this small detail much of Tess's predicament is foreshadowed: she will be caught between convention and her instincts. The problem Tess will experience is the problem faced by all his major characters: they cannot fit into society, yet they have to live in society and consequently they are punished for their waywardness.

Wayward, however, seems the wrong word for Tess. That is the word society would use in condemning her, but Hardy seems to write from another angle. In calling her a 'mere vessel of emotion' he emphasises how she is ruled by the heart and feelings, and likely to be lacking in a certain social calculation. When he goes on to mention how her mouth had not yet 'settled into its definite shape' this suggests her youthfulness but also a fluidity about people which is eventually shaped, and probably restricted, by the social roles they are forced to play. But the overwhelming sense I get from this passage is of Tess as physically vulnerable. This is primarily due to the way in which Hardy dwells on small physical details, such as the colour on her cheeks, her eyes growing moist, the pouted-up mouth, and her lower lip. The effect of this is to create a delicate sense of the heroine, the concentration on all these small details of her body encouraging us to feel sympathetic, even protective, towards her. A look at just this one passage has already begun to add to our sense of the novel: it can be seen that Hardy does not just deal with how society treats Tess but also provides a very involving picture of Tess as victim.

Yet, although Hardy's sympathies seem entirely with Tess, he is always ready to admit the importance of social attitudes. Tess is very much a member of society: her pride is affronted by her father's behaviour and the comments of the other girls. The constant dilemma of Hardy's characters can again be seen here: they are emotional and sensitive people, yet they are also characters who have to live in society and who share conventional social feelings.

(3) Select a second passage for discussion

After a first look at Tess, you might want to look at one of the men in her life. Any scene featuring either Alec or Angel would repay analysis, but the particular passage I have chosen is Angel's first appearance in the novel which comes just after the passage quoted above. He is seen standing with his two brothers:

> The eldest wore the white tie, high waistcoat, and thin-brimmed hat of the regulation curate; the second was the normal undergraduate; the appearance of the third and youngest would hardly have been sufficient to characterise him; there was an uncribbed, uncabined aspect in his eyes and attire, implying that he had hardly as yet found the entrance to his professional groove. That he was a desultory tentative student of something and everything might only have been predicted of him.
>
> [p. 43]

Can you see how Angel is being presented as a man apart in some way? Hardy works from visual impressions, and with Angel's brothers confidently sums up their social roles from their appearance, but Angel has not yet slotted into a social role. If he were to adopt a career, society would put him in a kind of uniform, but at the moment he is young and rather unformed. It is again the case, then, that the novel is declaring its theme of the conflict between social conformity and the inherent nature of people. Yet what strikes me about Angel here is that he is presented as a rather featureless characterless youth, as if he is just waiting to find his social role. Tess, by contrast, is always presented as having a rich natural personality. The difference between them is reflected in the language employed to present them: a cold, rather intellectual style is used for Angel – as in 'desultory tentative student' – whereas a far warmer style is used for Tess – 'for all her bouncing womanliness, you could sometimes see her twelfth year in her cheeks'. The language used to describe Angel tends to be awkward, angular and hard, whereas what Hardy repeatedly stresses in his descriptions of Tess is a kind of fluid, natural shape. From this scene alone, therefore, we can anticipate the hard, conventional response Angel will make to Tess's declaration of her 'past'.

(4) Select a third passage for discussion

In the simplest terms, what the novel presents is a dramatic confrontation between the social and the natural, between society and Tess. The most dreadful example of the abuse of Tess's innocence is when she is raped by Alec D'Urberville. He is accompanying her home late at night. Tess, after a long day, is extremely tired:

> Only once, however, was she overcome by actual drowsiness. In that moment of oblivion her head sank gently against him.
>
> D'Urberville stopped the horse, withdrew his feet from the stirrups, turned sideways in the saddle, and enclosed her waist with his arm to support her.
>
> This immediately put her on the defensive, and with one of those sudden impulses of reprisal to which she was liable she gave him a little push from her. In his ticklish position he nearly lost his balance and only just avoided rolling over into the road, the horse, though a powerful one, being fortunately the quietest he rode.
>
> 'That is devilish unkind!' he said. 'I mean no harm – only to keep you from falling.'
>
> She pondered suspiciously; till, thinking that this might after all be true, she relented, and said quite humbly, 'I beg your pardon, sir.'   [p. 104]

There is a great difference between the words and behaviour of Tess and the words and behaviour of Alec. He is cynically calculating: look at the slow, angular deliberation of the sentence describing how he manoeuvres himself on the horse to take advantage of her. Tess, by contrast, is so drowsy that she is not in control of her movements. Tess, who 'sank gently', is again presented in soft terms, whereas Alec, calling her 'devilish unkind', is hard and aggressive. He is thinking and calculating; Tess, on the other hand, acts on 'a sudden impulse'. When Alec rapes her it is a brutal violation of natural innocence. It could be argued on the basis of all this that Hardy has made the theme at the centre of his novel much more pointed than in any of his earlier works. He always presents characters at odds with society, but never before has he presented society in such condemnatory terms, and never before has he sympathised so totally with the victim of society's brutality and insensitivity. Yet the forcefulness of the content is accompanied by extraordinary delicacy in the writing, as must be evident in these passages considered so far, and in particular in the way we are made to feel for Tess in her predicament. In addition we are made aware that the issues are far from simple. Alec D'Urberville, seen as a rich man taking advantage of a vulnerable employee, might stand as a graphic example of the abuse of what is natural, but the complicating twist is that Alec is also motivated by something dark and perverted in his own nature. Hardy never loses sight of the fact that nature can be cruel as well as attractive.

(5) Select a fourth passage for discussion

The main line that I have found myself developing in this analysis of
Tess of the D'Urbervilles is that while the overall plot of the novel is very
simple and the bias of Hardy's sympathies very clear, Hardy creates
something extremely delicate and subtle within this simple frame.
These twin qualities of the novel – its directness and delicacy – should
be apparent in any passage I look at. Just at random I have selected
this paragraph where Hardy is commenting on Tess's refusal to
marry Angel:

> At such times as this, apprehending the grounds of her refusal to be her modest sense
> of incompetence in matters social and polite, he would say that she was wonderfully
> well-informed and versatile – which was certainly true, her natural quickness, and
> her admiration for him, having led her to pick up his vocabulary, his accent, and
> fragments of his knowledge, to a surprising extent. After these tender contests and her
> victory she would go away by herself under the remotest cow, if at milking time, or
> into the sedge, or into her room, if at a leisure interval, and mourn silently, not a
> minute after an apparently phlegmatic negative.   [p. 216]

We can see here again the broad opposition which is always at the
forefront of the novel. There is a strong contrast between the social
reasoning of Angel and the instinctive actions of Tess. My impression
is that *Tess of the D'Urbervilles* is structured on this opposition in a very
direct way; the idea is always present, with various image oppositions
being used to emphasise it. The one I have emphasised most so far is
the opposition of hard and soft, which is again in evidence here, but
you might find other repeated images which help illustrate and define
the issues in the novel. For example, Hardy sets vertical images
against horizontal images, so that what man builds on the land
appears as at odds with what lies naturally with the land.

What really makes the novel special, however, is, I think, what
Hardy conveys within this clear frame. The paragraph above starts
with Angel's view of Tess's reasons for refusing him: he believes that
the reasons must be social, that she must be worried about the class
difference. At no point does he consider that there might be some
more personal reason. The coldness of his reasoning is reflected in
Hardy's use of a hard, abstract style and an elevated vocabulary, with
phrases such as 'apprehending the grounds.' When the paragraph
switches to Tess's feelings, the sentence structure immediately
becomes simpler, and everything is concrete rather than abstract.
What is most impressive, however, is the extraordinary way in which

Hardy presents her response: she goes off to milk the 'remotest cow' or off into the sedge, as if she just wants to absorb herself into a world of nature which is quite removed from all the tribulations of the thinking world. It is as if Angel belongs to the world of words and rational thought, whereas words cannot really define Tess's feelings and so her response is presented in visual terms. And, very often, the most touching moments in the novel are when Hardy presents a visual picture of Tess, or of Tess's actions, as she finds herself in conflict with society's reasoning.

The pressure on Tess all the time, however, is that she cannot retreat into a world of nature, she has to live in the social world. Her natural instinct simply to love has to be reconciled with society's ideas about love and marriage; and although Hardy might sympathise totally with Tess, he does not just protest at the cruelty of society but presents a convincing picture of the reality of Tess's dilemma.

(6) Have I achieved a sufficiently complex sense of the novel?

I am reasonably satisfied with my progress as I do seem to have put together a view of what the novel is about and why it is so impressive. If you were to look at a series of passages you might reach quite different conclusions from mine, but that is how it should be. I am not offering my response as a correct view of the novel, just trying to illustrate how you can work from a series of passages to build a view of a novel.

What I have not dealt with yet, however, is how Hardy finishes the story. It might prove most helpful if I comment briefly on three episodes from the latter stages of the novel. First, Tess's decision to live with Alec: the text never really explains Tess's reasons, but this is consistent with what I have established about the novel as a whole. No doubt a social explanation could be given, but the novel has forcefully suggested that Tess's actions are primarily instinctive, and so cannot therefore really be explained in words. It is the same when she murders Alec: the actual moment is not presented and there is no description of Tess's feelings. But this again seems consistent with Hardy's theme: sociological and psychological explanations could be given, but the whole drift of Hardy's novel seems to be that there is an opposed natural world, which operates by different, rather incomprehensible, rules. This is again apparent as the police close in on Tess at the end of the novel. She is asleep; in line with the novel as a whole, it is as if a rational day-time consciousness is in conflict with a sleepy, irrational quality in nature and people. Tess is the embodiment of this spirit; Hardy can picture Tess and her predicament, but he cannot presume to explain in rational language what is going on in her mind. This is why, when you have read the novel, what might well stay with you more than anything else is a strong visual sense of the heroine and the memory of a number of powerful visual moments.

II Aspects of the Novel

If Hardy's readers were asked to vote on which was their favourite Hardy novel, I am sure that *Tess of the D'Urbervilles* would emerge as a clear winner. It is an extraordinarily powerful and moving work. Yet, surprisingly, some critics do find fault with it, and, even more surprisingly, examination questions, while acknowledging its force, often ask candidates to consider its limitations. The essence of the objections is a belief that Hardy is too heavy-handed and insistent. Unsympathetic readers point to the clumsiness of the story in which everything is contrived to go wrong for Tess. They also criticise the outbursts against fate, and the stereotyped characterisation of the men who misuse Tess; the argument is that Hardy has sacrificed credibility in order to get his point across. What redeems the novel for such readers is the portrait of Tess herself, the way in which we are deeply involved with her on her journey through life and the way in which Hardy conveys her heroism.

This might, of course, be a fair reflection of your feelings about the novel. You might admire the presentation of Tess but feel that the note of social protest in the work is too strident. Such an opinion on its own, however, does not amount to a critical response. If you wanted to take this line you would have to work from passages which enabled you to express this response to the novel. It might be the case, however, that you greatly admire the vigour of Hardy's social criticism, in particular his sense of how Tess is at the mercy of male values. Again, though, you would need to work from specific passages showing how they lead you to take a certain view of the novel.

It could be argued, however, that we belittle Hardy's achievement if we focus too much on *Tess of the D'Urbervilles* as a work of social protest, and equally that we underestimate the true range and force of the work if we focus too much on Tess. The best way of illustrating this is if we now look at several more passages, concentrating this time on the subtlety of Hardy's writing. Indeed, this is the most effective way of countering any suggestions that Hardy is at all heavy-handed as a novelist. Rather than bothering to counter each individual objection to his work, it is much better to take a positive approach, demonstrating from the evidence of the text itself just what a marvellous writer he is. The rest of this section, therefore, takes a closer look at **how Hardy writes**. Search for a passage you like, a passage where you think the writing is interesting or attractive. I chose this scene which takes place a couple of years after the death of Tess's baby. She and Angel are working on a farm and a relationship is beginning to develop between them. Hardy describes the farm at daybreak on a foggy summer morning:

> Or perhaps the summer fog was more general, and the meadows lay like a white sea, out of which the scattered trees rose like dangerous rocks. Birds would soar through it into the upper radiance, and hang on the wing sunning themselves, or alight on the wet rails subdividing the mead, which now shone like glass rods. Minute diamonds of moisture from the mist hung, too, upon Tess's eyelashes, and drops upon her hair, like seed pearls. When the day grew quite strong and common-place these dried off her; moreover, Tess then lost her strange and ethereal beauty; her teeth, lips, and eyes scintillated in the sunbeams, and she was again the dazzlingly fair dairymaid only, who had to hold her own against the other women of the world.   [p. 171]

To my mind it is absurd to suggest that any author who writes as beautifully as this could possibly have any limitations, but this is an expression of an opinion rather than criticism; we need to look closely at the passage.

Remember that a passage of description is never included just to fill up space, that it always reflects the central concerns of the novel. This passage deals with both the farm and Tess, but it might be easier if we start with Tess. What I think is central is the contrast between how Tess appears in the early morning and how she appears in the full light of day. She is beautiful by daylight – a 'dazzlingly fair dairymaid' – but at dawn she appears almost magical – she is associated with precious objects, such as diamonds and pearls, and Hardy writes of 'her strange and ethereal beauty'. What is conveyed is a sense of a special, natural quality in people. This quality in Tess is associated with nature itself. As Hardy describes the farm there is little sense of anything solid: everything is foggy and dreamy, and the meadows appear like a sea. It is an indefinite, intangible world. There are times when the novel shows us the darker, more destructive idea of nature, but what I think is primarily conveyed in this novel is a sense of nature as unregulated. It is extremely beautiful but defies being caught and pinned down. This obviously has parallels with Tess, and what is also clear is that Hardy's prose has to rise to the challenge of presenting something so elusive. The principal device used is imagery, so this passage is dazzling with light shining through the fog. The images also suggest fragility, and small delicate moments: look, for example, at 'now shone like glass rods' and 'minute diamonds of moisture'. It all combines to create the sense of something fragile, delicate and elusive, yet beautiful and precious.

This is the kind of delicacy we find everywhere within the strong frame of this novel. Why, you might ask, do some readers fail to see this? How can they accuse Hardy of being heavy-handed? The answer, I think, is that such readers are judging the work purely in realistic terms; they are considering whether Hardy offers an accurate mirror image of life. And, viewed from that angle, the novel could be said to have limitations. What I am suggesting, however, is that Hardy offers us something more exciting than a mirror image of life, that he always writes with a sense of a force in life which is elusive and cannot be explained. Those who suggest that his work has limitations focus so much on the accuracy or credibility of the social picture presented in the novel that they lose sight of this whole richer dimension of Hardy's writing, in which he creates a powerful sense of the force of nature and human nature as limitless, elusive, tantalising and marvellous. In short, they declare that Hardy is writing a social protest novel and find it wanting, whereas the actual texture of Hardy's writing suggests that, although there is a strong note of protest in his novel, his most extraordinary ability is to create and convey a sense of a natural energy at work in life.

Hardy's descriptions of Tess and nature provide the delicacy in the novel; what provides the drama is nature clashing with society. Just such a moment occurs when Tess tells Angel about her past life:

The pair were, in truth, but the ashes of their former fires. To the hot sorrow of the previous night had succeeded heaviness; it seemed as if nothing could kindle either of them to fervour of sensation any more.

He spoke gently to her, and she replied with a like undemonstrativeness. At last she came up to him, looking in his sharply-defined face as one who had no consciousness that her own formed a visible object also.

'Angel!' she said, and paused, touching him with her fingers lightly as a breeze, as though she could hardly believe to be there in the flesh the man who was once her lover. Her eyes were bright, her pale cheek still showed its wonted roundness, though half-dried tears had left glistening traces thereon; and the usually ripe red mouth was almost as pale as her cheek.   [p. 280]

As always there is delicacy within a bold pattern. The bold pattern is the hardness of Angel confronting the softness of Tess. Yet the picture is humanised by Hardy telling us that Angel 'spoke gently'; a moment later, however, the mention of his 'sharply-defined face' insinuates the idea of the sharp and defined force that the soft and elusive Tess is up against. As is so often the case in Hardy's novels, he seems to write in two different styles at once: he can see things from a social viewpoint, interpreting things as any member of society would, yet he also acknowledges forces and actions that are beyond rational comprehension. For example, he pictures Tess touching Angel but can only speculate on what her feelings were. The most obvious way in which his writing creates this sense of something intangible is by the constant use of nature imagery, so even in these few lines the relationship of Tess and Angel is compared to the ashes of a fire, and her touch is compared to a breeze.

The conclusion we can draw from the passage is that Hardy's subtlety and effectiveness as a writer is again apparent. We are offered a complex sense of the relationship between the ways of society and the freer spirit of nature. What is also apparent here, as is so often the case in this novel, is how Hardy emphasises the sense of Tess as fragile and vulnerable. He focuses on small physical details, such as her eyes and pale cheek, so that we sympathise with the trials of such a delicate woman in such a hard world.

The main point I have made so far in this section is that Hardy is not just writing a novel of social protest. The novel is partly that, but his real energies go into creating the sense of the force that strains against social convention. As this is a natural force, it might be a good idea to take a direct, if brief, look at **Hardy's presentation of the natural world** and his **use of natural imagery**. It is easy to find a relevant passage to discuss as images of the natural world and descriptions of the landscape are everywhere in the novel. I have selected a passage where Tess having parted from Angel is rambling the countryside and sleeps out one night. She hears what appears to be the sound of suffering animals:

Directly the assuring and prosaic light of the world's active hours had grown strong she crept from under her hillock of leaves, and looked around boldly. Then she perceived what had been going on to disturb her. The plantation wherein she had taken shelter ran down at this spot into a peak, which ended it hitherward, outside the hedge being arable ground. Under the trees several pheasants lay about, their rich plumage dabbled with blood; some were dead, some feebly twitching a wing, some staring up at the sky, some pulsating quickly, some contorted, some stretched out – all of them writhing in agony, except the fortunate ones whose tortures had ended during the night by the inability of nature to bear more.

Tess guessed at once the meaning of this. The birds had been driven down into the corner the day before by some shooting-party; and while those that had dropped dead under the shot, or had died before nightfall had been searched for and carried off, many badly wounded birds had escaped and hidden themselves away, or risen among the thick boughs, where they had maintained their position till they grew weaker with loss of blood in the night-time, when they had fallen one by one as she had heard them.   [pp. 323–4]

I think the main thing about this passage is that Hardy is clearly drawing a parallel between the fate of Tess and the fate of the birds. The birds have been hunted, and have taken refuge in the depths of the wood. In exactly the same way, Tess, whom we see emerging from the 'hillock of leaves' in which she has taken refuge, is a victim. The way in which Hardy writes about Tess here is probably true throughout the novel; it seems reasonable to assume that she will constantly be associated with the natural world and nature's creatures.

There is, however, another aspect to this passage and one which raises again the question of whether Hardy is too heavy-handed and insistent in making his protest. It could be argued that the comparison between Tess and the hunted birds is rather obvious and laboured, that Hardy is ramming a message down our throats. Similarly, some readers might suggest that Hardy's symbolism is heavy-handed: he mentions the blood on the plumage of the birds. From the moment Tess's horse is killed in an accident at the beginning of the novel, Hardy constantly returns to this image of blood, in particular the shedding of the blood of the innocent. That is the negative response to this passage. I prefer, however, to take a positive approach, and what I would suggest is that those who criticise Hardy just pick up the ideas and do not pause long enough to consider the extraordinary quality and delicacy of the writing.

What strikes me here, and I am sure that this is true throughout the novel, is the concrete and visual force of everything presented. The abstract theme in the novel is how Tess suffers as a consequence of the moral views of the society in which she lives. But Hardy constantly presents a physical sense of Tess as a tangible person physically experiencing assaults and misuse. When Alec and Angel mistreat her,

Hardy writes less about her thoughts than how their cruelty is revealed in her appearance. In the same way, what, to me, transforms this passage from a simple protest to something vivid and powerful is the way that Hardy sticks with and describes fully the physical suffering of the animals, and their appearance. This is obviously emotionally involving, but it also seems to fit in with the whole tenor of his theme in the novel: we are made to feel that the world of feelings, and instincts, and immediate sense experiences – indeed the whole of natural life – is something that is more immediate, more valuable, and more true than the world of abstract reasoning, and of social philosophies. The text is consistently and insistently concrete and visual in the pictures it presents; this deepens the social protest force of the work immeasurably, as we not only grasp the points being made, but feel the physical reality of nature and of suffering people.

Generally then, what we can reasonably assume to be the case in the novel is that Hardy presents a very physical, strongly visual sense of Tess and nature, and that he will constantly associate Tess with everything natural. Soft, poetic imagery will often be used for Tess and nature, just as hard, prosaic imagery will be used for the social world (in the passage above look at how Hardy describes how the 'prosaic light of the world's active hours had grown strong . . .': in 'prosaic', 'active' and 'strong' the characteristics of the social world are simply but effectively suggested). Rather than elaborate the point in general terms, though, it should prove far more productive simply to look at another passage where nature features prominently. It is again the case that, as nature is always central, just about any passage would do, but I have picked a passage from fairly late in the novel where harvesting is taking place. Traditionally harvesting might seem a joyful time of the year, when mankind and nature are in harmony, but as presented in this scene most of the joy has gone:

> The old men on the rising straw-rick talked of the past days when they had been accustomed to thresh with flails on the oaken barn-floor; when everything, even to winnowing, was effected by hand-labour, which to their thinking, though slow, produced better results. Those, too, on the corn-rick talked a little; but the perspiring ones at the machine, including Tess, could not lighten their duties by the exchange of many words. It was the ceaselessness of the work which tried her so severely, and began to make her wish that she had never come to Flintcomb-Ash.   [p. 374]

The pattern of society and the pattern of nature are again at odds; society has adopted a machine as more efficient and productive, but it seems cruel and life-destroying. It is again the case, however, that what really brings Hardy's idea to life is the physicality of his description. It is apparent in the way that working on this machine is shown to be physically unpleasant for Tess, so that she is 'perspiring' and severely tried. But it is also there in the way that Hardy consistently presents us with a visual impression of everything. For example, he does not just tell us that things used to be different, but presents us with the picture of the men with flails and 'the oaken barn-floor': we again, therefore, get an impression of an immediate, sensory world. The idea all the time is of a natural shape and order (which was 'slow' and soft – a word such as 'winnowing' suggests its soft quality) which has been supplanted by an imposed, unnatural shape: it is a hard existence – they 'could not lighten their duties' – and totally at odds with any natural rhythm of working, as suggested by the idea of 'the ceaselessness of the work' now.

What many people remember from *Tess of the D'Urbervilles* more than anything else is a picture of Tess as victim, but what these passages discussed above have led me to believe is that much of the novel's unique quality lies in its physical and visual descriptions and its imagery. Of course, I might be quite wrong. The validity of my reading of the evidence is, however, neither here nor there, as all I want to get across in this book is that if you look closely at short extracts of the text you should receive enough impressions to build your own coherent case about a novel. My examination of the evidence has led me to develop a certain line of argument, but you should try to have the confidence to build your own views from your own examination of the passages you choose to discuss. As with Hardy's other novels, you might want to think about this work as a tragedy, or consider the role of fate, or look at the social picture it presents, but I hope that by now it is clear how all these issues inter-relate: how Hardy is always concerned with the meeting place between the rational and irrational, between the social and the natural. But if you take that as your premise, it is your examination of a number of passages that will allow you to fill out your own sense of how Hardy develops his standard concerns in this particular novel.

6

Jude the Obscure

I Constructing an overall analysis

THE main idea in this book is that the best way to approach a Hardy novel, or indeed any novel, is to try and see a pattern in the work as a whole and then to look at a number of passages, interpreting them in the light of the pattern you have detected. The simplicity of this approach might have become obscured at times as I have also tried to illustrate some of the lines of interest that you might pursue in a Hardy novel, but in this chapter I return to basics. I am not trying to construct any kind of elaborate case about *Jude the Obscure*; I just want to demonstrate how a look at the evidence of the text enables you to build your own view of a novel. The place to start, as always, is with some thoughts about the pattern you can see in the plot.

(1) After reading the novel, think about the story and what kind of pattern you can see in the text

Jude Fawley, a young man with a passion for learning, hopes that one day he might get into university but has to forget his plans when Arabella Donn traps him into marriage. They are not suited to each other, however, and soon separate. Jude then turns to his studies again, but the university is not interested in the aspirations of this working-class man. Jude at this point in his life meets his cousin, Sue Bridehead, and soon falls in love with her. Sue, however, marries a schoolmaster, Phillotson, but this is another unsuccessful marriage and Sue flees from her husband. She and Jude start living together; they both obtain divorces but Sue is reluctant to marry Jude. They have two children and are joined by Jude's son by Arabella. Disaster ensues: Jude's son, called Father Time, murders the two younger children and then hangs himself. Sue, overwhelmed with feelings of guilt, returns to Phillotson. Jude goes into a decline, drifts into the company of Arabella again, and, in the closing pages of the novel, dies.

With the plot of any novel, think first about how it presents the relationship between the principal characters and the society in which they live. The first thing that might strike you about Jude is that he wants to succeed in society: the summary starts by mentioning his aspirations to get into university. Almost immediately, however, things begin to go wrong. He makes an unwise marriage and he and Arabella soon separate. Hardy, as always, is presenting a character who finds it difficult to fit into the pattern of ordinary life. Even Jude's desire to go to university can be seen in this light: he is unhappy in the role in which he finds himself and wishes to change things. He is presented, then, as a young man at odds with the conventions of society. This becomes even more evident when he meets Sue. Sue feels trapped in marriage; her own individuality rebels against the restraint of marriage, and she finds her appropriate partner in Jude. *— not so*

What is more difficult to understand and make sense of is the *Arabella's* sequence of events at the end of the novel beginning with Jude's son *and* killing his brother and sister and himself, yet our general ideas should help again. What we can say is that this is the kind of calamity that can happen when individuals find themselves so far outside the social fold; the shock of the murders panics Sue into returning to Phillotson, but Jude dies alone, now totally alienated.

In the novel as a whole, then, what we see is two individuals who because of their temperaments find themselves at odds with society. The idea of a society versus nature tension can help us define this more precisely. What we might say is that both Jude and Sue are controlled by the instability of their own natures; they follow the vagaries of their temperament rather than disciplining themselves to accept the sort of compromises people normally make in society. Nature, of course, always has a wild and destructive side, and Jude's son's self-destructiveness is terrifyingly clear, but there is also something self-destructive about the whole behaviour of Jude and Sue: following their own natures they seem to be intent on courting disaster. *due to bad marriage luck hereditary — superstition*

(2) Select a short passage featuring one of the main characters and try to build upon the ideas you have established so far

So far we have looked for a pattern in the work as a whole; your sense of the text will, however, only really begin to come to life as you look at specific incidents and passages, starting with a look at one of the main characters. I decided to look at Jude, and the passage that caught my eye is this one where, as a boy, he is working as a human scarecrow with the job of frightening off the birds:

> The boy stood under the rick before mentioned, and every few seconds used his clacker or rattle briskly. At each clack the rooks left off pecking, and rose and went away on their leisurely wings, burnished like tassets of mail, afterwards wheeling back and regarding him warily, and descending to feed at a more respectable distance.
>
> He sounded the clacker till his arm ached, and at length his heart grew sympathetic with the birds' thwarted desires. They seemed, like himself, to be living in a world which did not want them. Why should he frighten them away? They took upon them more and more the aspect of gentle friends and pensioners – the only friends he could claim as being the least degree interested in him, for his aunt had often told him that she was not. He ceased his rattling, and they alighted anew.
>
> 'Poor little dears!' said Jude aloud. 'You *shall* have some dinner – you shall.'
>
> [*Jude the Obscure* (New Wessex edition, 1974) p. 34]

As I have stressed throughout this book, the key to interpreting a passage is to look at it in the light of the ideas you have already established. Here, for example, you might start by considering Jude's very uncomfortable relationship with nature, as suggested by his job as a human scarecrow. There seems something harsh and unnatural about his job, something that is suggested in the contrast between the hard 'clack' of Jude's rattle and the birds rising on 'leisurely wings'. There is a 'wheeling' freedom about the birds as against the position Jude has to occupy. What this suggests to me is a hostile relationship between society and nature, as if society is inimical to everything natural.

Jude himself reacts against the task that society requires of him. Hardy's choice of phrase here is interesting. We are told how Jude felt sympathetic to 'the birds' thwarted desires'. It might have been enough to mention Jude's sympathy, but the mention of desires draws our attention to that passionate, instinctive side of life that society tries to restrain. This fits in which the wider pattern of the book where we can point to the function of marriage as the central institution by which society attempts to regulate love and desire. These human feelings, however, cannot easily be controlled. Early in the book, for example, Jude is seduced by Arabella's physical charms and yields to the desires of the flesh. Often, as when Jude stops frightening the birds here, there is something attractive about such undisciplined, rash actions. Again, Jude's sympathy for the birds is also attractive: he sympathises with what is gentle and vulnerable, with the fragile things that society seeks to damage and destroy. That is a description that we could equally apply to Jude and Sue themselves, seeing them as vulnerable people at the mercy of a harsh, judging world. Another side of Jude, however, which I sense from the way in which he talks to the birds in this scene, is that there is something very naive about him, and that he might exasperate us because of his inability to act in a reasonable and sensible way. Or at least, that is how I see it; but one of the central points I have been trying to get across in this book is that your reading of the evidence might lead you to draw quite different conclusions. That, of course, is how it should be: all that matters is that you do work from the evidence and that, as you move from passage to passage, you try to build a coherent overall impression of the text.

(3) Select a second passage for discussion

At this stage you might want to look at Jude's relationship with Arabella. As always, find a passage for analysis: from the passage you would not only discover things about Jude and Arabella but also add to your sense of the concerns that permeate the novel as a whole. Instead of looking at Jude's relationship with Arabella, however, I have decided to look at Jude and Sue. Any scene in which the two of them appear would repay analysis, but I happened to come across a passage that occurs after Sue has run away from the training college where she has been preparing to be a teacher. She has crossed a river in her flight, and arrives at Jude's lodgings thoroughly soaked:

Jude put on her his great-coat in addition, and then ran out to the nearest public-house, whence he returned with a little bottle in his hand. 'Here's six of best brandy,' he said. 'Now you drink it, dear, all of it.'

'I can't out of the bottle, can I?'. Jude fetched the glass from the dressing-table, and administered the spirit in some water. She gasped a little, but gulped it down, and lay back in the arm-chair.

She then began to relate circumstantially her experiences since they had parted; but in the middle of her story her voice faltered, her head nodded, and she ceased. She was in a sound sleep. Jude, dying of anxiety lest she should have caught a chill which might permanently injure her, was glad to hear the regular breathing. He softly went nearer to her, and observed that a warm flush now rosed her hitherto blue cheeks, and felt that her hanging hand was no longer cold. Then he stood with his back to the fire regarding her, and saw in her almost a divinity.

[p. 165]

One way to start thinking about this passage is by considering the whole situation and how it has come about. Ask yourself why Sue has run away from the training college. In some way it must have seemed like a prison to her, and therefore she has fled from it. She has come to Jude's lodgings, and by the standards of the day there must be some impropriety in an undressed young woman being in his room. These are the kinds of details in the text that signal to us that these are characters at odds with the conventional social order.

Yet they remain members of that social order. Sue, for example, has been presented as a very unconventional young woman, but she cannot commit the unladylike act of drinking out of a bottle. This might seem a trifling detail, but there is much in the novel which is in the same key: Jude and Sue always feel worried, even guilty, about their unconventional behaviour. But one thing that comes across clearly here, and is again evident in the novel as a whole, is how kind and caring they are in their feelings for each other. The whole time there is a softness about their actions, as in 'He softly went nearer to her': they appear as 'soft' characters in a 'hard' world. And as always in Hardy's novels there is a stress on the physical vulnerability of such people. Notice how Hardy focuses on little physical details, such as Sue's voice faltering and her head nodding, and how this makes us feel the vulnerability of people who are buffeted between the harsh laws of society and the trouble they create for themselves because of the wilfulness of their own natures.

All these details are important, and there might of course be others that I haven't spotted at all, but probably the most memorable detail is the closing phrase: Jude seeing 'in her almost a divinity.' It is a phrase that could be interpreted in various ways; all I will suggest is that it draws attention to the pursuit of something almost religious by Jude. It is as if the alternative to the harshness of society is an ethereal, natural, transcendent ideal, perhaps an ideal of love unfettered by any social restraints. But Hardy is not preaching in his novel. He is less concerned with providing visions of how things might be in an ideal world than with showing the reality of how even the most idealistic characters are caught in everyday life. This comes out again in one other fine detail: look at how Hardy says that a warm flush 'rosed' Sue's cheeks. This association of Sue with a natural object, specifically here a flower, adds to our sense of natural characters caught in the restraints of society. Society condemns the relationship of Jude and Sue, but the text manages to suggest that it is soft, caring and natural.

(4) Select a third passage for discussion

Just as she ran away from the training college, so Sue runs away from marriage to Phillotson, and at that point the real relationship with Jude commences. It is a complex relationship; indeed, if you tried to sum it up your comments would soon appear general and inadequate, and this is another good reason for working from the evidence of the text. You might not be able to say everything that could be said about their relationship, but your comments will have some precision as a result of being based upon a concrete piece of evidence. I have picked a passage where the two, by now both divorced, have fallen on hard times and are having to sell their furniture. They overhear people talking about them:

> They soon found that, instead of the furniture, their own personal histories and past conduct began to be discussed to an unexpected and intolerable extent by the intending bidders. It was not till now that they really discovered what a fools' paradise of supposed unrecognition they had been living in of late. Sue silently took her companion's hand, and with eyes on each other they heard these passing remarks – the quaint and mysterious personality of Father Time being a subject which formed a large ingredient in the hints and innuendos. At length the auction began in the room below, whence they could hear each familiar article knocked down, the highly prized ones cheaply, the unconsidered at an unexpected price.
> 'People don't understand us,' he sighed heavily. 'I am glad we have decided to go.'
> 'The question is, where to?'
> 'It ought to be to London. There one can live as one chooses.'   [p. 325]

In the passage, then, Jude and Sue overhear people talking about them as they wait for the auction of their possessions. Can you see how the passage suggests that they live, or have been living, in a world of their own? It is only now that they begin to realise how the world at large regards them. Their first response is to move on, but that won't always be possible for they are members of society whether they like it or not and will eventually have to face the consequences. There are simple things that they have to take account of, for example they need to earn a living in order to survive at all, but part of the pressure on them will always come from themselves. They are nagged, and will be nagged, by feelings that they should conform. Or, at least, that is the case with Sue. To anticipate the rest of the story, Sue by returning to Phillotson will accept the rules of society even though they make her unhappy. Jude, however, will increasingly become convinced that freedom is all-important, and will at the end of the novel die alienated and an outcast.

We can see, therefore, the broad way in which the themes are developing, but as in any novel what makes the novel memorable is the way in which things are brought to life on the page. In this passage, for example, what strikes me most of all is the touching physical detail: 'Sue silently took her companion's hand.' There is something very moving in that small gesture of human contact in a harsh and unfriendly world. What, though, also comes across in this extract is the innocence of this pair, that they really don't know how people feel about them, that they seem to think that the goods with the most sentimental value will somehow carry the greatest cash value. This impractical, detached aspect of Sue and Jude is evident more generally in the novel in, for example, the frequency with which they seem to miss trains; it is as if, in a society that runs according to schedules and time-tables, they cannot cope with such things at all.

(5) Select a fourth passage for discussion

It would be possible to go into the relationship between Jude and Sue in far greater detail, and if you were studying the novel for an examination you would probably want to look at several of the scenes in which they both feature. What always will be evident, however, is that Jude and Sue move along, for better or for worse, in an uncomfortable relationship on the fringes of society. They are happy in a way, but also unhappy. They cannot settle down in the social framework, and, as every scene in which they appear is likely to suggest, there is something unstable about them that makes them attract disaster. This, it could be said, is the destructive side of unregulated nature which is always there as the complement of the attractive side of nature.

Jude and Sue, then, drift along, permanently insecure and anxious. And might continue to do so, except for the shock of an event which destroys everything and which forces a change in their lives: this is the murder of the other children by Father Time and his own suicide. Some readers argue that this incident is so unlikely that it spoils the whole novel, but before passing judgement you should look closely at the evidence trying to decide what Hardy is trying to achieve in this episode. I have picked out a short sequence where the bodies are actually discovered:

> He saw that the door of the room, or rather closet – which had seemed to go heavily upon its hinges as she pushed it back – was open, and that Sue had sunk to the floor

JUDE THE OBSCURE   71

just within it. Hastening forward to pick her up he turned his eyes to the little bed spread on the boards; no children were there. He looked in bewilderment round the room. At the back of the door were fixed two hooks for hanging garments, and from these the forms of the two youngest children were suspended, by a piece of box-cord round each of their necks, while from a nail a few yards off the body of little Jude was hanging in a similar manner. An overturned chair was near the elder boy, and his glazed eyes were slanted into the room; but those of the girl and the baby boy were closed.

Half paralysed by the strange and consummate horror of the scene he let Sue lie, cut the cords with his pocket-knife and threw the three children on the bed; but the feel of their bodies in the momentary handling seemed to say they were dead. He caught up Sue, who was in fainting fits, and put her on the bed in the other room, after which he breathlessly summoned the landlady and ran out for a doctor.   [p. 355]

This is an extraordinary and grotesque scene, and it is difficult to know how to respond. This is in part due to Hardy's method, that, as so often, he presents us with the visual impression and leaves us to interpret the material for ourselves. But it should be possible to work something out which is consistent with the ideas about the novel that we have developed so far. Let me stress that the following interpretation is just my response; if your ideas about the novel had developed along a different path from mine you might well respond to this scene in a quite different way. Some readers, for example, dismiss it as crude: they say it shows Hardy as tired and bitter, creating a crude scene to hammer home the point that society destroys people's lives.

I think, however, that the scene is more subtle than that. The family have been presented for many pages as social outsiders, and Little Jude has already come across as a weird child who displays none of the normal characteristics of any ordinary youngster. Consequently, it could be argued that in Little Jude we see something of the stranger and more disturbing side of nature. He is a child who by temperament can understand only extremes and cannot grasp how people continue to live together. He leaves a note: 'Done because we are too menny'. Society for all its shortcomings does, it must be said, always try to accommodate everyone: society has rules simply because rules enable everyone to live together. The child's act, by contrast, is closer to nature in the raw. This is, I think, part of the subtlety of Hardy, that he might sympathise intensely with social misfits, and understand the misery of their position, but he also understands why people bond together in societies for safety and security. Indeed, after this event Sue returns to Phillotson: it is as if misery within the social framework is in some way preferable to a dangerous life on the fringes of society. But for Jude there can be no return: isolated and alienated, he dies alone.

(5) Have I achieved a sufficiently complex sense of this novel?

This novel, it could be argued, examines, as all of Hardy's novels seem to do, a persistent tension between society and nature. This theme is, however, developed in different ways in the individual novels, and in addition each individual reader will see and interpret the issues with an emphasis of his or her own. The whole point in building your own response from a number of passages is to try to define this distinctive impression of your own, so that you really manage to sort out and articulate your response to a novel.

One of the things that strikes me, for example, is that whereas *Tess of the D'Urbervilles* constantly associates Tess with nature, and thus presents her as a pure and innocent force in the social world, *Jude the Obscure* emphasises different things. The main impression of Jude and Sue that comes across is of highly-strung, sensitive, nervous people. The way in which Hardy presents the heroines helps account for this difference between the two novels: Tess, for the most part, seems healthy and blooming whereas Sue seems thin, fragile and easily hurt. Along with Jude, she seems delicate and sensitive. *Jude the Obscure* might in some ways seems to be no more than a novel in which Hardy protests at the restrictions on people's lives, but a novel of protest becomes something altogether more complex when it has such complicated central characters. Much of the complication of the novel arises from Hardy's perception that what is natural might be warm and loving, but that nature can also be perverse and cruel, and both Jude and Sue unintentionally make the other suffer. What, then, to my mind, makes Hardy a complex novelist is his recognition of the complex nature of the tensions between society and nature; what makes him a moving novelist, however, is his sympathy for the characters caught between society and nature, including their own natures.

You, of course, might disagree. Or you might feel that you couldn't deduce so much so quickly from such a small amount of evidence. But this isn't a problem: the answer is to keep on looking at passages until things do fall into place, until a sharp, clear and full sense of the novel comes together in your mind. I am aware of gaps in my own analysis: I really need to find out more about both Jude and Sue, and a closer look at Arabella, Phillotson and Little Jude would be rewarding in itself and help fill out my ideas about the novel. I hope by now, however, that the way to tackle matters is plain. The only worthwhile approach is to keep on looking at passages, as only the evidence of the text can help you sort out your response to the text.

II Aspects of the Novel

Jude the Obscure could be discussed in all kinds of ways. It is yet another novel by Hardy which could be called a tragedy, and it also has something significant to say about social change in Victorian England: what is most noticeable in this respect is that the usual farming background of a Hardy novel has all but disappeared, and that Wessex appears as a gloomy, bleak and barren place. It could be argued that Hardy starts from a position where the old natural order has been eradicated, that there is only the rigid order of society, and that there is no place for 'natural' characters such as Jude and Sue in this new world.

I do not, however, want to pursue any specific theme in the second half of this chapter. The other chapters should provide ideas about some of the angles from which *Jude the Obscure* can be discussed. All I want to do here is look at the texture and detail of Hardy's writing in a couple of passages. The reason for doing this is to reinforce the point that I have been making all along, that the best way to explore the text as a whole is to see how Hardy develops his ideas and themes in particular passages. I want to illustrate just how much can be found in a couple of short extracts.

These are not special extracts, just passages selected at random, passages that caught my eye when I opened the book. The first is a scene describing Jude looking at Sue in her house. He looks through the window:

A glimmering candle-light shone from a front window, the shutters being yet unclosed. He could see the interior clearly – the floor sinking a couple of steps below the road without, which had become raised during the centuries since the house was built. Sue, evidently just come in, was standing with her hat on in this front parlour or sitting room, whose walls were lined with wainscoting of panelled oak reaching from floor to ceiling, the latter being crossed by huge moulded beams only a little way above her head. The mantelpiece was of the same heavy description, carved with Jacobean pilasters and scroll-work. The centuries did, indeed, ponderously overhang a young wife who passed her time here.

She had opened a rosewood work-box, and was looking at a photograph. Having

contemplated it a little while she pressed it against her bosom, and put it again in its
place.   [p. 227]

Very often it is the case that an extract will tell you very directly what
the passage is about and what the larger concerns of the novel are, and
that is certainly the case here. The narrator tells us that it is about
how the centuries 'ponderously overhang a young wife who passed
her time here.'

The other details of the passage fill out what Hardy means by this.
We see Sue trapped in this room just as she is trapped in marriage to
Phillotson. Everything that bears down on her is heavy whereas Sue
comes across as light. There is such a sense of heaviness that the room
has sunk over the centuries: the whole weight of the past, and
convention, and the rules of society are weighing down on Sue. What
you might also notice is the attention Hardy gives to the oak
panelling in the room, and, as with all details, this can be made sense
of in terms of our society versus nature opposition. The point here
seems to be the unnaturalness of the room, as if nature has been
reduced to the role of providing mere decoration.

The simple point I am making throughout this section is that all the
details can be interpreted in the light of a society versus nature
opposition, but when we begin to notice the immense amount of
significant detail in a passage we realise both how Hardy brings his
themes to life and also the complexity of his themes as he develops
them. Look at the second paragraph: Sue keeps a photograph of Jude
in a box. It is a rosewood work-box, again seeming to suggest the idea
of something natural being reduced to the status of a domestic
artifact. But Sue's behaviour is the more interesting point: I feel that
for all her talk of being an independent woman, the idea of freedom
frightens her, and that she feels rather frightened by Jude as a man.
The idea of keeping his photo in the box therefore manages to suggest
how she likes to keep things contained, framed and packaged, as if she
feels safer with the image of the man than with the man himself.

There are other points that could be discussed in this extract – for
example, the way in which Jude is peering in on Sue: Hardy's novels
are full of scenes where people spy on others in this kind of way. It is as
if everybody, ultimately, occupies their own private world and we can
only intrude upon individual experience. I don't, however, want to
discuss every aspect of the passage but only to get across the idea that
complexity of detail in a passage points to compexity in a novel as a
whole, for the details articulate in all kinds of ways the concerns at the

heart of the novel, providing all kinds of differences of emphasis and nuances of meaning in a work.

Another passage should provide further proof of this. Just a few paragraphs before the previous extract, Jude, who has been to visit Sue, is taking his leave of her and she speaks to him from a window:

Now that the high window-sill was between them, so that he could not get at her, she seemed not to mind indulging in a frankness she had feared at close quarters. 'I have been thinking,' she continued, still in the tone of one brimful of feeling, 'that the social moulds civilisation fits us into have no more relation to our actual shapes than the conventional shapes of the constellations have to the real star-patterns. I am called Mrs Richard Phillotson, living a calm wedded life with my counterpart of that name. But I am not really Mrs Richard Phillotson, but a woman tossed about all alone, with aberrant passions, and unaccountable antipathies . . . Now you mustn't wait longer, or you will lose the coach. Come and see me again. You must come to the house then.'

'Yes!' said Jude. 'When shall it be?'

'Tomorrow week. Good-bye – good-bye!' She stretched out her hand and stroked his forehead pitifully – just once. Jude said goodbye, and went away into the darkness.   [p. 226]

Let's take this detail by detail. First, why is Sue in the window and why does Hardy mention the high window-sill between them? My response is that Sue feels safer when she is in the orderly frame of the window; she might reject convention, but she needs some frame and structure to her life. In a rather similar way, the high window-sill is a kind of sexual barrier between them. So Sue feels safer framed in the window, and with a wall between her and Jude.

She then begins to speak, and what she says is a very direct statement of the larger themes we have been exploring, for she states that although labelled as Mrs Richard Phillotson, this name gives no sense of her real self. She is talking about how something free and natural is restrained by social convention. But look at the odd, awkward way in which she speaks; the very oddness of it, however, signals to us that she is an outsider, that she does not speak as most people speak and therefore does not relate to society in the kind of way that other people can. Some readers are irritated by the way in which Jude and Sue are forever analysing their feelings and by their sensitivity about seemingly everything. Look, however, at the interpolation in Sue's speech where Hardy writes how she spoke 'in the tone of one brimful of feeling'. The intellectual quality of her speech, which might annoy, is humanised by the emotional stress of this. It is this kind of detail, almost a physical detail, that makes us feel for the character caught in the situation. And that lightness and delicacy is continued when she reaches out and strokes Jude's head.

At the end Jude goes away into the darkness: this again contributes to the overall effect. It is as if for a moment Jude and Sue can create a little, positive area of light. Society might batter them and nature has its darker side, but in these moments of contact this couple can achieve something natural and spontaneous, even if fragile. Or at least, to make the point I have made throughout this book, that is how I see it. The evidence of the text might lead you to draw quite different conclusions, but remember that your arguments must always develop from the evidence of the text. This will take time as you will need to ponder over the passages you select for analysis, but it is time well spent. A critical book can only provide you with someone else's view of the text, but if you look at the text for yourself you can't help but develop your own views. In addition, as the next chapter explains, you will be acquiring a stock of material that you can use directly and effectively in essays.

7

Writing an essay

ONE of the things that makes studying English unlike studying any other subject is that success depends upon your ability to write a good essay. Tell yourself from the start, therefore, that you are going to produce really good essays, essays that examiners will want to praise rather than find fault with. But how can this be done? Isn't the ability to write well a gift that some people are born with? It's worth pausing to consider the thinking behind such a view: the informing assumption is that essay writing is largely a matter of luck and inspiration, and that a good essay cannot be planned and calculated in advance. The first thing to get clear, however, is that inspiration has very little to do with producing good essays; the basis of good essay writing is having a method that enables you to write good essays.

If you haven't yet discovered a method for yourself, what I can do here is steer you towards a productive approach. The advice I give will differ from the advice other people, including teachers, might give you, but not to any substantial degree, as the basic rules of essay writing are beyond dispute. It all starts with appreciating what you are trying to do in an essay: this can be summed up in the formula that **in a critical essay you are trying to build a clear argument from the evidence of the text**. That is a simple formula, and the method of your essay should be equally simple. What the essay says can be complex and difficult, but the overall design and movement of the essay should be simple. But how is it possible to achieve this kind of well-organised essay? Well, there is obviously no point in just sitting down, starting to write and hoping that things will work out all right. Before you start, you need to understand the question, and know roughly what shape your answer is going to take; this doesn't mean knowing 'the answer', but knowing roughly how many paragraphs you are going to write and roughly how long they are going to be.

The rest of this chapter explains all of this more fully, but it might be a good idea if I summarise the main points here at the outset just to get across the idea of how simple the method of a good essay can, and indeed should, be. Recognise that you are being asked a question and this means that you will have to argue an answer. There is no sense in trying to give your complete answer in the first paragraph of your essay; if you do, you won't have any other points to make or go on to, and you will almost certainly tie yourself up in knots by trying to say too much too soon. Use your first paragraph just to clarify what the issue is that you are being asked to consider.

Once you have got to grips with the question, there is only one place to find the answer: in the text. So, start your second paragraph by turning to a specific scene (I'll explain the mechanics of how to do this later). Try to establish something central to the question from this scene. When you have done so, you can conclude this paragraph, and proceed to another paragraph, again working from a specific scene or passage in the text. Build your essay in paragraph blocks; try to see how each paragraph establishes a step in an argument. By the time you have looked at five or six episodes, and discussed them in the light of the question you are considering, a clear argument should have developed. And you will have achieved the aim of an essay: you will have built a clear argument from the evidence of the text. The rest of this chapter merely repeats this advice at greater length, making reference to a specific question.

The question

Teachers and examiners set questions; most students fail to answer the questions set. That might seem absurd but it is true. Asked a specific question about Henchard in *The Mayor of Casterbridge*, most examination candidates will pour out everything they know about him. So, make sure that you answer the question set. In order to do this, you need to realise that questions confront you with a problem or an issue to discuss. Take this example of a question on *The Mayor of Casterbridge*:

To what extent, if at all, do the characters in *The Mayor of Casterbridge* remain constant as their circumstances change?

There is no single correct answer to this question. You could argue that they do change, or that they remain constant, or that some of them change. But the very fact that different views can be taken should make it clear that you will have to argue a case in your answer, proving that case from your reading of the evidence of the text.

Another thing to grasp is that there is no such thing as an easy question or a difficult question. The question I have given here might seem relatively simple, and this in itself might deceive students into thinking that their answers can be loose and chatty. The point to realise about questions, however, is that they are always asking you about the central issues in the novel. In order to help you organise your answer the examiner selects a particular aspect of the work – in this instance, characters – and you must concentrate on this aspect, but your answer must be informed by a larger sense of the work. This might seem frightening, but it's not: all the earlier chapters of this book have stressed the importance of seeing a broad pattern in a novel. This is what I mean here by 'a larger sense of the work'. In this question on *The Mayor of Casterbridge*, you are being asked to consider whether **the nature of the characters** changes **as their social circumstances change**. If, as in this example, you can see that the question reflects the larger nature versus society opposition in Hardy's novel, then this will give your answer a sense of direction and purpose: you will see that the question bears on the whole subject of the novel and that more is required than just a description of the characters.

The first paragraph

If you cannot sum up the question in the way described above, don't worry about it. You don't need to sort everything out before you start because an essay itself should help you discover the answer. Use your first paragraph merely to define the issue involved in the question. For example, an opening paragraph on this question might read as follows:

In *The Mayor of Casterbridge* we see dramatic changes in the lives of all the principal characters. This is most true of Henchard who at the opening of the novel is unemployed, then rises to become mayor, but who at the end of the novel is isolated and alone. Farfrae also experiences great changes, coming to Casterbridge as a poor man and rapidly making his fortune, and there are also great changes for Elizabeth Jane who finds her father, only to discover that he is not her father after all. The question, however, is whether the characters themselves change as their circumstances change. A closer look at some of their experiences should help reveal the answer.

Can you see how, in this short paragraph, I have done just enough scene-setting to make it clear what I am talking about, and have asked, but not attempted to answer, the main question? A first paragraph should be as short and to the point as this. If you find yourself rambling on it will almost certainly be the case that you are losing the thread of what you are saying, and failing to define clearly the subject of your essay.

The second paragraph

Using paragraphs effectively is probably the central secret of writing good essays. I've already talked about the need for a clear first paragraph which is to the point and gives a sense of the direction you are going to take. Each subsequent paragraph should also be disciplined and serve a purpose. Look at it this way: in your opening paragraph you will have identified the issue for discussion; your closing paragraph will wrap things up. In between you need five or six paragraphs of about half to two-thirds of a page in length. Each will represent a step forward in your answer to the question and make a distinct advance on the previous paragraph. If paragraphs are too short, the ideas will be skimpily expressed. If the paragraphs are too long, you will lose the thread of what you are saying. An examiner can tell a lot about an essay just from looking at its appearance: if an essay is constructed in seven or eight paragraphs, and the five or six central paragraphs are all of a fairly standard length, then the examiner will be surprised if the answer is disappointing, as such a clear lay-out almost guarantees clear thinking.

As your second paragraph begins, turn to the text. A second paragraph on the question we are using might begin: 'We first learn something of the character of Michael Henchard when we see him getting drunk at the fair and selling his wife.' In the course of this book I have quoted lengthy extracts from novels, but obviously this is not practical in an essay. What is practical, however, is to describe vividly the incident you have in mind. After that, start to discuss what you can see in the scene. What you are looking for are points relevant to the question: this early scene from *The Mayor of Casterbridge*, for example, conveys a sense of how hot-headed and intemperate Henchard is, but you have got to describe how this specific scene creates this impression of the character. After referring to the text, and having discussed a scene, you will need to pull the threads of this paragraph together. This is vitally important; at the end of a paragraph you must stand back and sum up what you have established so far. With Henchard, you might review your progress and say that Hardy offers us a sense of Henchard as a very strong and domineering personality, a man who seems to resent all restraints on his freedom, even the restraint of marriage. The passage examined, therefore, has established something about the strong nature of this man.

Always make sure that you do sum up at the end of a paragraph in this kind of way, forcing yourself to write two or three sentences of conclusion. This will ensure that you are answering the question, and help push along an argument in your essay. The concluding sentences should also trigger off your next paragraph. For example, the logical starting place for our next paragraph on Henchard would be that, having seen the strength of his personality, we want to see whether he changes as the novel progresses. And the way to find out is to choose a scene from later in the novel which looks as if it will help you answer the question.

I hope it is clear how the method described here can be used for any question about Hardy: the approach to take at all times is to build your argument from the evidence of the text. Another relevant point to remember is that an essay should be self-sufficient. You are trying to persuade the reader of your essay, trying to convince the examiner. Consequently, it serves no purpose to say something like 'the incident on page 143 proves that . . .' A page reference proves nothing; you have got to convey a sense of the text, so that the reader of the essay feels that he or she is confronting the evidence from which you are drawing your conclusions. This might also be a good place to mention style. Quite simply, don't worry about style. If you are conveying a vivid sense of the text and then making your points clearly and logically, then your style will be vivid and persuasive. What you must worry about, however, is writing in grammatical sentences. Nobody expects every sentence to be perfect, but a sentence that rambles on and on won't make sense. All of this is largely a matter of thinking about what you are doing: it is better to think about what a sentence says rather that gabbling out sentences as quickly as possible. People only write badly when they don't think about what they are saying and don't order their thoughts.

The third paragraph

Each paragraph should trigger off the direction in which you head in the next paragraph, so in *The Mayor of Casterbridge*, searching for a scene where Henchard is at the centre of the action, you might choose the episode where Henchard comes up to greet the royal personage visiting the town and is man-handled by Farfrae. Again describe the scene, then comment on everything in it that strikes you as relevant to the question. You might be able to remember certain phrases or certain little details: it is the way in which you make use of these that will really bring your answer to life. In this scene, for example, you could make a great deal of how Farfrae grabs hold of Henchard's lapel. Then, at the end of the paragraph, again devote two or three sentences to pulling the threads together and drawing a conclusion. What you might decide about Henchard, for example, is that, although he has come down in the world, he is still as hasty and extreme as ever. As your answer progresses, providing you take care to sum up at the end of each paragraph, you should discover that you are getting hold of the larger issues in the novel. What you might already realise by this stage is that Henchard's essential nature is not changing. This is the point I have made throughout this book, that there is a natural force in Hardy's central characters which is indifferent to society's rules and so is constantly at odds with society.

Continuing to build

The questions to ask yourself at the start of each paragraph are: 'Is there another aspect to this question that I have not considered yet?' and 'Is this the whole story, or is there something that contradicts what I have said so far?' Consequently, answering our question on *The Mayor of Casterbridge*, at this stage you might try to find evidence that Henchard does change, or you might decide to go on and consider some of the other characters. I will pursue the second of these options here. You might consider Farfrae: select a suitable scene and describe it. What does the scene tell you about Farfrae? You might, in the same paragraph, look briefly at another scene to see if he changes. That is quite all right: you don't need to stick rigidly to a 'one scene to a paragraph' format. But do be sure that you draw the threads together at the end of the paragraph: for example, you might decide that the novel presents Farfrae as a canny, calculating man, and, even though he has a romantic side to his nature (as seen in his love for Lucetta), he never really alters. So, end your paragraph with a conclusion: be careful never to end a paragraph with a quotation. You have always got to come in at the end of a paragraph and establish your control of the argument.

In the fifth paragraph of your essay you might consider Elizabeth Jane. Look at the evidence: decide for yourself whether she changes. I think the kind of conclusion I might reach, but only after looking closely at a scene or two, is that, as a result of experiencing unhappiness in her life, Elizabeth Jane is keen to distance herself from the extremes of nature and lead a settled social life. What matters, however, is what the text leads **you** to believe.

Changing direction

If at all possible, it is a good idea to alter the direction of your essay about two-thirds of the way through. In the case of our sample question, you might have devoted four paragraphs to building the idea that Hardy presents a view of human nature as essentially unchanging. But it will add interest to your essay, and probably do more justice to the book, if, about two-thirds of the way through, you suggest that the issue is more complicated than this. What in effect is happening is that the earlier stages of your answer have established a broad view of the novel, but now, in the last third, you can start to look for complications in the text. If that is a bit difficult to understand, let me illustrate how to put together two paragraphs on Henchard that run in a different direction from the paragraphs we have produced so far.

As always, start by picking a scene, such as the picture of Henchard alone on the heath. Discuss the scene: you might discover yet more evidence of how he rejects society, but you might also come across evidence of how Henchard attempts to understand himself as he thinks about his experiences and life in general. And so there is a change in Henchard: he has become more reflective upon the human condition. This is, in fact, a predictable change in Henchard who like all tragic heroes matures as he confronts experience, and emerges as heroic in his bravery in facing up to life.

You might pick another scene, such as Henchard and Elizabeth Jane together in the novel. Henchard might appear as anti-social as ever, but the evidence of the text might suggest to you that he is desperate for Elizabeth Jane's love. That obviously complicates matters: most of the time Henchard appears entirely self-sufficient, but it could be argued that he recognises, or at least we as readers come to feel, his need for companionship and love. Can you see then that it can be argued that Henchard does change? As I have said already, if you can alter the direction of your argument in the last third, or start seeing another side of the case, then that adds a whole additional level of interest to your essay.

The concluding paragraph

You might feel embarrassed about writing your concluding paragraph as, having been firmly in control all along the way, there should be nothing now left to say at the end. But what might happen is that, having managed to write a really clear and well-controlled answer, you might find that the words begin to flow in this last paragraph as you sum up the answer to the question, the answer you have finally arrived at.

Use the format of the essay to help you solve the problem

This is all very well, you might say, but the question I have to answer is far more tricky than the question considered above. The whole point of this chapter, however, is to argue that the same method will help you answer any question, and answer it really well. Indeed, this essay format should help you sort out an answer. Let us assume that you have been asked to consider nature imagery in *Far from the Madding Crowd*. Your first paragraph can suggest that, as the novel is set in the country, a lot of nature imagery can be expected, but as yet the significance of that imagery is unclear. Then, in paragraph two, look at a scene. With something as specific as nature imagery you might want to quote two or three lines. On the basis of this passage you should be able to establish a first point in your argument. Consideration of more scenes will then push your argument along, provided that you remember that each paragraph must advance on the paragraph before. In the last third of an answer on nature imagery, you might, in order to change direction, switch to considering the darker side of nature. Really it is a case of reducing the essay to logical steps, and then building your answer in logical steps. Yet what is so good about this kind of systematic approach is that it should allow you the freedom to express and develop your own ideas, and convey your enjoyment and appreciation of a text. In other words, having a clear essay method allows you to be inventive and enthusiastic and original because you know that you are building a solid and sensible argument from the evidence of the text.

8

Discussing an extract

THE previous chapter offered some ideas about how to tackle a conventional essay question. Increasingly, however, examiners are setting another type of question where they present a lengthy extract from a novel and then ask you to write about the novel, basing your ideas mainly, but not exclusively, on the evidence of the passage. A lot of examination candidates find this kind of question awkward to answer, and, indeed, at first you might find it hard to see how to go about it. What will obviously help you is if you have a method, a way of organising your answer, and it is this that I try to provide in the following pages. In order to make everything as clear as possible I will work from a specimen question. The question is about *The Return of the Native*, but is typical of the kind of question that might be set on any of Hardy's novels:

Referring in detail to the passage given, examine the picture of Eustacia just before her death, relating this to the earlier presentation of her character. What responses does Hardy try to evoke in the reader and what means does he use to this end?

Eustacia at length reached Rainbarrow, and stood still there to think. Never was harmony more perfect than that between the chaos of her mind and the chaos of the world without. A sudden recollection had flashed on her this moment: she had not money enough for undertaking a long journey. Amid the fluctuating sentiments of the day her unpractical mind had not dwelt on the necessity of being well-provided, and now that she thoroughly realized the conditions she sighed bitterly and ceased to stand erect, gradually crouching down under the umbrella as if she were drawn into the Barrow by a hand from beneath. Could it be that she was to remain a captive still? Money: she had never felt its value before. Even to efface herself from the country means were required. To ask Wildeve for pecuniary aid without allowing him to accompany her was impossible to a woman with a shadow of pride left in her: to fly as his mistress – and she knew that he loved her – was of the nature of humiliation.

Any one who had stood by now would have pitied her, not so much on account of her exposure to weather, and isolation from all of humanity except the mouldered remains inside the tumulus; but for that other form of misery which was denoted by the slightly rocking movement that her feelings imparted to her person. Extreme unhappiness weighed visibly upon her. Between the drippings of the rain from her umbrella to her mantle, from her mantle to the heather, from the heather to the earth, very similar sounds could be heard coming from her lips; and the tearfulness of the outer scene was repeated upon her face. The wings of her soul were broken by the cruel obstructiveness of all about her, and even had she seen herself in a promising way of getting to Budmouth, entering a steamer, and sailing to some opposite port, she would have been but little ·more buoyant, so fearfully malignant were other things. She uttered words aloud. When a woman in such a situation, neither old, deaf, crazed, nor whimsical, takes upon herself to sob and soliloquize aloud there is something grievous the matter.

'Can I go, can I go?' she moaned. 'He's not great enough for me to give myself to – he does not suffice for my desire! . . . If he had been a Saul or a Buonaparte – ah! But to break my marriage vow for him – it is too poor a luxury! . . . And I have no money to go alone! And if I could, what comfort to me? I must drag on next year, as I have dragged on this year, and the year after that as before. How I have tried and tried to be a splendid woman, and how destiny has been against me! . . . I do not deserve my lot!' she cried in a frenzy of bitter revolt. 'O, the cruelty of putting me into this ill-conceived world! I was capable of much; but I have been injured and blighted and crushed by things beyond my control! O, how hard it is of Heaven to devise such tortures for me, who have done no harm to Heaven at all!'

[*The Return of the Native* (New Wessex edition, 1974), pp. 371–2]

The most difficult thing about discussing a passage such as this is that you are going to have to do a lot of thinking in the examination, as you must respond to the specific passage set. Unfortunately, many students duck such a challenge and just pour out their prepared notes. In this case, for example, many examination candidates would simply put down everything they knew about Eustacia without even bothering to read the passage carefully. That, it must be made clear, would be a complete waste of time: you will only gain marks if you discuss the passage actually set.

What will help you do this is if you go into examination feeling confident that you can relate any passage set to the text as a whole, and that you can see the wider concerns of the novel in the details of the passage. In order to have this sort of confidence you need to have a general strategy for coming to terms with a Hardy passage, and I will talk about this next. But what you also need is to be able to write a good essay about the passage, and so, in the rest of the chapter, I offer some ideas about how to shape and organise your response.

Understanding the extract

As I have argued throughout this book, you should be able to find a tension at the heart of any passage, a tension that you can relate to the larger concerns of the novel. The most obvious tension to search for in Hardy's novels is a society versus nature opposition, so when you are confronted by a passage in an exam it makes sense to start looking for such a tension. With this passage, for example, my impression is that we see Eustacia caught between society and nature, but perhaps being absorbed into, or overwhelmed by, nature. She has desired to escape from the Heath into polite society, but here we see her battered by the storm, and also torn apart by the strain in her own mind.

Just saying that means I have already detected the wider concerns of the novel in the particular passage under discussion, and it is this that you need to do at the start. Don't start your thinking about the passage on a narrow front, but instead approach it by way of the broad themes of the novel, trying to see how Hardy is exploring these themes through Eustacia. The idea of a society versus nature opposition will help you get a strong grasp on a passage, and that initial strong grasp will give your whole answer authority and direction as you will have a broad frame in which it should be possible to respond sensibly and sensitively to the details. It should never prove difficult to see the larger themes implicit in a passage: as I have argued throughout this book, a society versus nature tension of some kind will always be in evidence in the text. If you can see the large pattern behind a passage, that gives you a solid basis from which to build your answer.

Organising an essay

Let us assume that you have read the passage you have been set and have managed to see how society and nature are at odds in the text. It might be, as in this passage from *The Return of the Native*, that you are going to have to deal with a character such as Eustacia who, despite her social aspirations, will never really fit in with society; a character who, with his or her unstable nature, is more at one with the larger instability of nature. But even if you can see all this, you do need a method that will enable you to translate your perceptions into a clear and well-organised essay. And more than this: an essay where you manage to really convey something of your genuine feelings about and response to the text.

The first point to grasp in relation to this kind of question is that, just as much as on any other occasion, you are expected to construct and present a good essay. There is a tendency in writing about an extract to present a bitty list of points ('I noticed this, then I noticed this, and then there was another detail I noticed . . .'), but you have got to produce a well-crafted essay with shape, direction and purpose. As always with an essay, what you are really concerned with is building an argument from the evidence of the text. Therefore, everything that was said in the last chapter about constructing an essay in solid paragraphs, each of which advances the argument, applies just as much here. But getting the paragraphs in an essay to work depends upon getting the first paragraph right, so let's start at the beginning.

Don't try to say everything in the first paragraph of your essay. All you need to do in your first paragraph is say where the passage appears in the novel, state briefly what is happening in the scene, and then comment on the meaning or significance that you see in the passage. Here, for example, you might say that the scene appears late in the novel after Eustacia has left her home for the last time. It is her last appearance in the novel as a living person; within a matter of pages she will have died in the weir. What the passage deals with is Eustacia's desire to leave the Heath, but she seems trapped and caught. The passage then goes on to describe her state of mind, how she is confused and in turmoil, very much like the weather on the Heath itself. Such comments would provide you with the bulk of your first paragraph, but you must ensure that at the end you comment on the significance of the scene Hardy is presenting. This is a case of seeing the larger themes implicit in the passage. What I mean by this is seeing that it is not just a passage about an unhappy young woman: there's much more than character analysis involved. The easiest way of expressing these broader implications is to make use of the society versus nature pattern, how, in this passage, we see Eustacia aspiring to a settled life, but how she is trapped. But it is not only external nature that batters her but also the extremes of her own nature torment her, for she does not feel Wildeve is great enough for her. As is so often the case in Hardy's novels, then, we see someone who does not fit in with society caught uncomfortably between society and nature, including their own nature.

So far, then, if you employ the method suggested here, you would have looked briefly at the passage, but also have shaped a larger, controlling idea for your essay. It is at this point, however, that an answer could run out of control: it would be all too easy to go through the passage just listing every point that could be made without your answer really heading anywhere. Tell yourself, therefore, that your answer is going to have purpose and direction, and the best way to plan for this is to tell yourself in advance (as with writing a traditional essay) that you are going to have five or six central paragraphs in your essay, each a half to two-thirds of a side in length, and each advancing the case so that at the end of every paragraph you have advanced beyond the stage reached at the end of the paragraph before.

But what do you look at in each paragraph, and where do you start? The best advice is to go straight for details: don't try to say everything about the character or issue at once, but build from the details. So, in this passage, you have suggested in your first paragraph that Eustacia seems trapped by nature. You might start your second paragraph by mentioning how Hardy refers to 'her unpractical mind', and that this can be connected with facts such as her never having considered the importance of money before. You have found your details; now you need to relate them to a larger scheme of things. Do this by using the idea of a society versus nature tension that you set up in your first paragraph as a key to interpreting the details. So, for example, we can say that Hardy includes these details about Eustacia's 'unpractical mind' to suggest the romantic nature of her temperament, to show how she is a young woman who has never really come to terms with the mundane facts of life, covering everything from being aware of financial realities to accepting the constraints of marriage. Can you see how you can quickly move from the detail to a sense of Eustacia's character as a whole and the larger themes of the novel? What this kind of question also asks you to do, however, is refer elsewhere in the novel, and it is easiest if you do this on a regular, systematic basis. In the first half of a paragraph, work from a detail in the passage given, then shift to another scene in the novel which can be related to this in some way. You might pick out a scene where Eustacia is unhappy at home with Clym; again it will show her inability to fit in with society. But be precise when you refer to another scene: don't say, 'this aspect of Eustacia can be seen in her marriage to Clym', but do say 'this aspect of Eustacia can be seen in the scene where she and Clym . . .', and then go on to describe the precise piece of evidence that allows you to draw the conclusion. And, finally, as always, do remember to conclude, to sum up at the end of your paragraph, stating clearly what you have proved so far, even if it is only to say that we can see that Eustacia is a romantic, unpractical young woman.

That clear conclusion will set you up for advancing to a fresh point in your next paragraph. You now want to find another aspect, something you haven't really dealt with yet, so again, select details, and try to build from the details. You might pick up the way in which she tries to shelter under the umbrella, a point which emphasises the force of nature, its indifference and cruelty. What we see is Eustacia pathetically trying to protect herself against nature's extremes with an umbrella, something that belongs to the polite world of society but which is of no use on the Heath. Yet the passage also tells us that 'the chaos of her mind and the chaos of the world without' are very much the same, so we see again the desperate side of her nature. Again, in the second half of your paragraph, refer to another scene which reveals Eustacia's wildness, and the paragraph could then conclude with mentioning how the passage conveys to us the strength of natural forces in life, just how disruptive they can be.

We have now put together three paragraphs of an essay. Repeat the process in paragraphs four and five: 'Here are a couple of details from the passage; these details enable me to add to my impression of Eustacia's character; here is another scene in the novel which makes a similar point about Eustacia; on the basis of these examples, what I can now say about Eustacia is this.' It must be clear that the logic behind this approach is that the best way to arrive at a clear and comprehensive sense of the importance of Eustacia in the novel is to exploit an essay format that enables you to organise your impressions and that enables you to build your case steadily and persuasively.

There is, however, one part of the question that we have not yet touched, the part where you are asked to discuss 'what responses does Hardy try to evoke in the reader and what means does he use to this end?' A question obviously won't always be phrased in these terms; sometimes there won't be a subsidiary part to the question like this, and sometimes it might make a quite different request about what you are to discuss. However the question is phrased, though, you should try to add something fresh along these lines in the last third of your essay. As explained in the previous chapter, it alway makes an essay more impressive if you slightly alter direction two-thirds of the way through. When discussing an extract you can usually alter direction in the same way: having devoted the first two-thirds of the essay largely to discussing the content and themes, in the last third you can pay rather more attention to the distinctive way in which the author presents his material. This doesn't mean that you have to go in for a lot of technical analysis of his way of writing, but rather that you need to talk about the ways in which this is distinctively Hardy's way of writing. The earlier chapters of this book should give you all the necessary ideas about the kind of issues that you might want to discuss.

Here, for example, let us consider what we might include in the sixth paragraph of our essay. As always, start from the details of the passage. So far we would have established what Eustacia's dilemma is, and established a sense of the unsteadiness and romantic impulsiveness of her nature, but would probably also have seen how she is to be pitied in her plight. Now you might look at her speech in the last paragraph where she talks about 'the cruelty of putting me into this ill-conceived world! I was capable of much; but I have been injured and blighted and crushed by things beyond my control!' What we can say about this is that here we can see Hardy building up Eustacia as a tragic heroine: she asks those questions about the nature of experience that a tragic heroine almost invariably asks, and there are other things, such as her sense of her own potential, and her sense of the tragic waste of experience which add to this impression of her as tragic heroine. Can you see the substantial advance we have made here? We have moved forward from discussing character and content to a sense of how Hardy is presenting his heroine as tragic. Obviously, in the second half of this paragraph, it would be a good idea to refer closely to another scene where Eustacia comes across as a tragic heroine. And so this paragraph could conclude with a statement that Hardy wants us to feel a certain awe at his heroine, a feeling that is created by his use of the kind of ambitious language that signals tragedy to the reader.

In the next paragraph you could again talk about Hardy's method. It might be that you decided to pick up the point explained in *The Mayor of Casterbridge* chapter of this book that Hardy's vision is never purely tragic, that he takes a social view as well. Here, for example, you might work from the details that help create a rather ambiguous sense of Eustacia: that she is a tragic heroine, but also a rather foolish, over-indulged young woman. But the thing about Hardy's method I want to pick up here is his stress on physical vulnerability, seen in his description of 'the slightly rocking movement that her feelings imparted to her person. Extreme unhappiness weighed visibly upon her.' As is so often the case in Hardy (and the rest of your paragraph would need to provide other examples from the novel), Hardy makes us feel for the character caught in the situation by conveying a vivid sense of the frail human form battered by the enormous force of the elements.

By this stage you would just need a brief conclusion to pull your essay together. But rather than go into that, let me just repeat the main points about how to tackle discussion of a long extract. As explained at the beginning of this chapter, you have got to be able to see the significance of the passage, but then you have got to be careful that you build a well-constructed essay. Employ a simple construction in each paragraph, looking at details and commenting on details, then referring to another incident in the novel that makes a similar point, and then, at the end of the paragraph, sum up what you have established so far. If you build an essay on this regular format it will be almost bound to be a good essay, but if you can slightly redirect the last third of your essay to press closer to your sense of what is really distinctive about Hardy's way of writing, then that will inject just that vital extra degree of interest and force into your answer. It will do so because it will show that you are alert to Hardy's writing and why he is such an enjoyable novelist to study.

A Note on Criticism

Before you start reading a lot of critical books about Hardy, indeed before you read any critical book, ask yourself why you are bothering to do so. Critical books are useful, but only if you use them in the right way. They should complement your own thinking about a text rather than serve as a substitute for thinking. The most important thing to remember is that your criticism will only stand up if it is based on your own impressions and experience of the text. It might be, however, that you just cannot see what a novel is about, that it leaves you totally baffled. At this point, a clear introduction to the novel which draws attention to its central themes can be very helpful. More often than not, the introductory essay in the edition of the novel you are using should prove illuminating in this kind of way. The introduction to the New Wessex editions of Hardy, published by Macmillan, and the introductions to the Penguin editions of Hardy are particularly good. Another useful purpose these introductions serve is if you want to verify your own response; it can be very encouraging to turn to a critical essay which shows that your own thinking about a novel is on the right lines. At the outset, if you are going to bother with criticism at all, don't search for unusual or eccentric criticism. What you need to establish is a solid and sensible grasp of the text, so stick to the kind of solid introductions I've listed above.

And really, if you can work out some big ideas about a novel you don't need to read any more criticism. Time spent looking at and thinking about passages from a novel is time much more usefully employed than time spent reading other people's views. But it might be that, even after doing a lot of work on the novel yourself, you still want to find out more. Indeed, working closely on a text might stimulate your interest to the point where you want to see how other people respond to the novel. This is the point at which it can prove useful to turn to criticism in order to add to or extend or even unsettle your own ideas. The two times at which it is most useful to look at criticism, therefore, are just after reading a novel, when you might need some help in sorting out your general ideas, and after doing a lot of your own work on a text, when you feel that your own thinking needs an additional stimulus.

The two books on Hardy which I have found most stimulating in this kind of way are *The Great Web* by Ian Gregor (Faber and Faber, 1974) and *An Essay on Hardy* by John Bayley (Cambridge University Press, 1978). They are very different but equally interesting: Gregor offers a very persuasive account of what is central in Hardy's fiction whereas Bayley's impressions are rather more piecemeal, but both critics are likely to spark off your own thinking. Critical books which include essays by a number of writers are also well worth looking at as they introduce you fairly quickly to different ways of looking at the same author. The two most notable books of this kind on Hardy are *Hardy: The Tragic Novels*, edited by R. P. Draper in the Macmillan Casebook Series (1975), and *Critical Approaches to the Novels of Thomas Hardy*, edited by Dale Kramer (Macmillan, 1979).

One thing that you might well realise if you start to read a lot of criticism of Hardy's novels is that critics lean towards certain views of him: some critics tend to emphasise the tragic pattern of his novels, others make more of the social picture he presents (particularly impressive in this respect is the section on Hardy in Raymond Williams' *The English Novel from Dickens to Lawrence*, Chatto and Windus, 1970), and there are others who concentrate on yet further aspects of his novels. I could provide a comprehensive guide to these critics, but do not feel that would be particularly helpful here. The books I have already mentioned cover all the main issues, but any book or article on Hardy particularly if published fairly recently, should add something to your own thinking. But if you do come across Hardy criticism in your library, try to read it sceptically, taking away good ideas if you can find them, but trying to see that every critic approaches Hardy from a certain angle and that any individual view of a great writer is bound to have limitations.

Remind yourself that the views of published critics are no more valid than your own, particularly if, in your own criticism, you always make a point of working closely from the text itself. And that is as good a way as any of judging the quality of any critical book you read: see if it sends you back to the text to explore it further for yourself.